Building Nonprofit Capacity

W9-ALL-437

Building Nonprofit Capacity

A GUIDE TO MANAGING CHANGE THROUGH ORGANIZATIONAL LIFECYCLES

John Brothers
and
Anne Sherman

JOSSEY-BASS
A Wiley Imprint
www.josseybass.com

Published by Jossey-Bass
A Wiley Imprint
989 Market Street, San Francisco, CA 94103-1741—www.josseybass.com

Library of Congress Cataloging-in-Publication Data

Brothers, John.
    Building nonprofit capacity: a guide to managing change through organizational lifecycles / John Brothers and Anne Sherman.
        p.   cm.
     Includes bibliographical references and index.
     ISBN 978-0-470-90777-1 (pbk.); ISBN 978-1-118-10326-5 (ebk); ISBN 978-1-118-10327-2 (ebk); ISBN 978-1-118-10328-9 (ebk)
        1. Nonprofit organizations—Management.   2. Organizational change.   I. Sherman, Anne. II. Title.
    HD62.6.B753   2012
    658.4'06—dc23
                                                                                    2011029152

Printed in the United States of America
FIRST EDITION
PB Printing   10 9 8 7 6 5 4 3 2 1

CONTENTS

Visit the Building Nonprofit Capacity
website at:

www.buildingnonprofitcapacity.com

We dedicate this book to the memory of our fathers,
John Brothers, Sr., and Warren T. Sherman, M.D.

ACKNOWLEDGMENTS

I begin first by thanking those individuals who helped in the development of this book, including reviewers and case study and interview participants. I also thank all the organizations with which I've worked. Realizing the missions and building the capacity of these important efforts is a true blessing.

I acknowledge my awesome wife, Arlene; my children, Max and Nina; and my dog, Lucy, for supporting me through this experience. I also give a special note to my mother and father's many unrecognized efforts, which I now greatly appreciate through my own experiences as a parent. Thank you.

—John Brothers

I am extremely fortunate to have worked for over eleven years at TCC Group, where I get to interact every day with smart and generous people who are deeply committed to the nonprofit and philanthropic sectors and to helping nonprofits increase their effectiveness. So much of the way I see the nonprofit world is a result of the training and mentoring I've received at TCC Group. Special thanks go to Pete York, Paul Connolly, Shelly Kessler, Richard Mittenthal, and Jared Raynor. Bonnie Mazza and Susan Misra have also made important contributions. Chantell Johnson and Sally Munemitsu are exceptional consultants, colleagues, and friends. Michele Garvey was a source of encouragement and good advice throughout.

It's been my privilege to work with nonprofit leaders who do brilliant and inspired work on a daily basis. The lessons in this book are the ones they've taught me. I am especially appreciative of Gary Bagley at New York Cares, Chet

Cantrell at Christian Activity Center, Becky Hatter-James at Big Brothers Big Sisters of Eastern Missouri, Cecilia Clarke of Sadie Nash Leadership Project, Rich Berlin at Harlem RBI, and Bob Rath of Our Piece of the Pie. Jane Donahue and Elizabeth George of the Deaconess Foundation in St. Louis are not directly quoted in this book, but have had a profound influence on my thinking about organizational lifecycles and what really helps nonprofits move "up the curve."

Given how much of the book talks about values, I would be remiss in not acknowledging my parents, Lyn and Warren Sherman, who have always modeled the importance of strong values for my siblings and me.

Finally, I thank Russell Langsam, because you changed everything. And Ben and Claudia Langsam, who make every day a lesson in lifecycles and adaptive capacity.

—Anne Sherman

We are both indebted to Allison Brunner, who helped get this project under way, and Alison Hankey at Jossey-Bass, who shepherded it through to completion. We are deeply grateful to David Campbell at the Department of Public Administration at the College of Community and Public Affairs at SUNY Binghamton, Paul Connolly at TCC Group, and Tim Wolfred at CompassPoint Nonprofit Services for their invaluable contributions as reviewers.

chapter ONE

Setting the Stage

Change as a Defining Force
in the Nonprofit Sector

First, introductions. We have between us over twenty-five years of experience working as consultants to nonprofits, foundations, and corporate funders. John is the owner of a firm called Cuidiu Consulting and is a senior fellow at the Support Center for Nonprofit Management, both based in the New York City area. Anne is an associate director and codirector of the strategy practice at TCC Group in New York City. Both of us spend our days helping nonprofit organizations understand how to increase their impact. We do this by providing a set of services loosely defined as "capacity building," which helps nonprofits (or the entities that fund them) function more effectively and efficiently, so that they can be as successful as possible in achieving their missions.

Between the two of us, we have worked with many nonprofits at various stages of development, presenting a wide range of strengths and challenges. We've both been fortunate enough to be part of efforts to get nonprofits off the ground. John has a great deal of experience at the other end of the lifecycle as well, having helped engineer nonprofit mergers to preserve the mission and value of programs after it had become clear that the organizations themselves were no longer sustainable. And both of us have worked with dozens of nonprofit organizations at all points in between "start-up" and "shutdown." Whereas Anne works more with established groups that seek to strengthen or grow, John does a heavy amount of his work with organizations that are either in the start-up phase or with groups that are in decline or turnaround. These groups include organizations with annual operating budgets of less than $100,000 and those with budgets of $50 million or more. As noted, we've worked with start-ups, and we've also consulted with nonprofits that are well over one hundred years old. Although we probably have the greatest depth of experience working with organizations that meet some kind of human service or educational need, our clients have also included art nonprofits, membership associations, and advocacy groups. We've learned a lot, and we're both keenly aware that we still have a lot to learn. What we enjoy most about our work is that it is never dull, stagnant, or repetitive.

In other words, it keeps changing.

To paraphrase a cliché, change is the one constant we can all count on, for better or worse. Has this ever been truer than during the present time, as we enter the second decade of the twenty-first century? Technology, globalization, a devastating economic recession that most would agree has put tremendous strain on nonprofits in the United States—these are just a few of the seismic shifts that have increased the pace of change for our sector. When we are called to help a nonprofit deal with some aspect of change, whether it's ostensibly positive ("We got the grant! Now what?") or negative ("Our executive director just gave two weeks' notice, and we have no clue how we're going to survive without him"), it's remarkable to us that our clients are frequently unprepared to anticipate, prepare for, or manage change, let alone serve as a catalyst of it. By and large, nonprofits are left to their own devices to manage the challenges and opportunities inherent in a change process, and, more significant, most are ill equipped to do so.

And to be sure, change isn't always something that is thrust upon an organization. Every day, nonprofit leaders are engaging in deliberate change efforts that they believe will enhance their ability to achieve mission—implementing a strategic plan, building a new layer of management, or adding a new program. For many of our clients, growth is a deliberate goal, often manifested in the expansion or replication of programs. Here too, it is our experience that many of our clients lack the tools or frameworks to help them succeed in their efforts.

Our intent in writing this book is to explore how to bolster the sector's capacity not only to weather change, but also to recognize the importance of change as part of a larger process of continuous improvement.

LIFECYCLE: A FRAMEWORK FOR INITIATING, ANTICIPATING, MANAGING, AND UNDERSTANDING CHANGE

There are many frameworks to help understand the concept of organizational growth and change; we decided to use the *lifecycle* as the model for this book. When we talk about a lifecycle, we mean a predictable pattern that most nonprofits will follow over time. Similar to the human lifecycle, the organizational lifecycle serves as a model for identifying and understanding a nonprofit's characteristics at a given point in time, assuming that most organizations will pass through a set of developmental stages. In this way, the lifecycle normalizes the difficulties of growth and change, putting them into a larger context, helping us understand where we are in a way that describes rather than judges.

The lifecycle model prescribes as well as describes, but also assumes that there is an optimal destination that all nonprofits should strive to achieve, and helps leaders understand what needs to be done in order to make the journey from point A to point B as successful as possible. It helps people focus on what needs to be done by putting strengths and weaknesses in context, normalizing them and saying that in fact the challenges of one phase might just be leading to further improvement.

We have both used variations of the lifecycle framework in our work, and here we offer an overview of those that we use in this book.

Susan Kenny Stevens: Bringing the Lifecycle Framework to the Nonprofit Sector

The organizational lifecycle is not a theory that originated with the nonprofit sector. The concept first emerged in the 1970s in the corporate sector, beginning with an article by Greiner in the *Harvard Business Review* titled "Evolution and Revolution as Organizations Grow" (1972). Over the next decade, the theory gained credibility. It wasn't until the 1990s that lifecycle theory took hold in the nonprofit sector. Susan Kenny Stevens began writing about nonprofit life-cycles in the early 1990s, and in 2001 published a book on the topic, *Nonprofit Lifecycles: Stage-Based Wisdom for Nonprofit Capacity*.

The Stevens lifecycle framework identifies seven stages, outlined here and illustrated in Figure 1.1:[1]

1. Idea: "There is no organization, only an idea to form one."

2. Start-Up: "An organization that is in the beginning phase of operation."

3. Adolescent (or Growth): "An organization whose services are established in the marketplace but whose operations are not yet stabilized."

4. Mature: "An organization that is well established and operating smoothly."

5. Decline: "An organization that is operating smoothly but is beginning to lose market share."

6. Turnaround: "An organization that is losing money, is short of cash, and is in a state of crisis."

7. Terminal: "An organization that no longer has a reason to exist."

Stevens's book represents perhaps the most influential thinking on the subject of lifecycles. In applying the lifecycle concept to nonprofits, Stevens

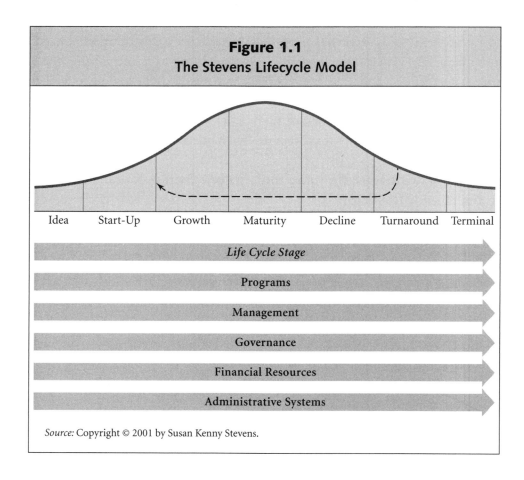

Figure 1.1
The Stevens Lifecycle Model

Idea   Start-Up   Growth   Maturity   Decline   Turnaround   Terminal

Life Cycle Stage

Programs

Management

Governance

Financial Resources

Administrative Systems

Source: Copyright © 2001 by Susan Kenny Stevens.

provides the sector with an important organization development framework. She was an early proponent of "right sizing" technical assistance and other types of capacity building activities, in that she recognized that this type of work is perhaps more complex than previously thought. Depending on where an organization is in its lifecycle, it will require different types of interventions or support. The changing nature of boards over time is a classic example: the board of a start-up tends to be more involved in the day-to-day work of the nonprofit and may be mostly made up of friends of the executive director (ED); as the organization matures, it becomes the board's job to pull back from operations and focus more on such tasks as fundraising and setting policy for the organization. There is no "board for all seasons," and understanding where an organization falls on the lifecycle can provide important clues as to the type of board that it needs, or needs to build.

Stevens also recognized that the lifecycle concept, though readily digestible, is fairly nuanced and complex. It is not a linear model: some nonprofits may follow the continuum Stevens establishes; others will not. Moreover, although most nonprofits can place themselves in a particular stage, it is also quite likely that aspects of an organization, such as programs, will fall into one phase of the lifecycle, whereas others, such as governance structure or management systems, will fall at a different point of development.

TCC Group: Lifecycle as a Journey Toward Increased Effectiveness

Early into the 2000s, TCC Group took a critical look at the lifecycle model, represented most frequently by the Stevens framework. In 2006, Paul Connolly, a senior vice president at TCC, published *Navigating the Organizational Lifecycle: A Capacity Building Guide for Nonprofit Leaders,* in which he noted that "A fully actualized, mature organization should remain vital and increasingly improve the quality of its programs—so as to make significant progress in fulfilling the defined need for which it exists."[2] A chronological trajectory is important and relevant, but misses at least one critical topic: organizational effectiveness, defined by TCC as *progress toward achieving mission.* If one considers achieving mission as the sector's prevailing "bottom line," programs and services are the primary ways in which nonprofits make that bottom line. High-quality, high-impact programs can be consistently delivered only if the organization has the proper infrastructure—board, staff, management systems, IT, financial systems, systems for evaluation and improvement, and so on.

Soon after the publication of Connolly's book, Peter York and Jared Raynor of TCC Group led the development of a lifecycle pyramid, implying an upward trajectory; its tiers correspond to phases of the Stevens model (see Figure 1.2).

The first phase is called "core program development"; an organization at this phase of the lifecycle needs to focus on the fundamentals—mission, organizational vision, and a coherent program strategy that reinforces mission in such a way that programmatic effectiveness is maximized. Think about it as organizational genomics—what is the DNA of a successful nonprofit, and how does one separate its core components? In the TCC Group model, core program offers an intrinsically linked system of mission, vision, and strategy. That is to say, programs relate directly to a shared set of organizational outcomes and reflect the most recent knowledge about "best practice." Core program takes up the most area of the pyramid by design. That is because nonprofits exist to fulfill their missions

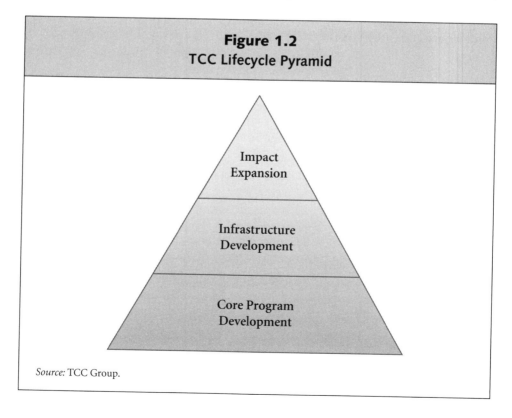

Figure 1.2
TCC Lifecycle Pyramid

Impact
Expansion

Infrastructure
Development

Core Program
Development

Source: TCC Group.

through high-quality, high-impact programs. No matter where a nonprofit falls on the lifecycle, staff and board leadership need to continually monitor and, as necessary, modify mission, vision, and program strategy in order to ensure maximum quality and effectiveness.

It is worth noting here that placement at the core program phase is *not* associated with an organization's age. Certainly, these are issues that start-ups grapple with, but we all know organizations that are far beyond start-up yet rightly belong in the core program lifecycle phase. These organizations would likely fall into the decline phase on the Stevens lifecycle; the TCC lifecycle assumes that in order to engage in effective turnaround, such an organization needs to first take a close look at its core program.

The second phase is called "infrastructure development" and assumes that once core programs have been established, the organization should make it a top priority to develop the infrastructure needed to sustain and perhaps even grow its programs. This phase is comparable to the adolescent phase of the Stevens model. The emphasis during this second phase is to ensure that the nonprofit has the systems and structures it needs to properly support its programs. The nonprofit that finds itself in the infrastructure phase isn't ignoring core program, but its program strategy is stable and successful enough that the organization can focus its attention on building its capacity. Capacity building efforts at this stage often focus on development of needed systems, such as human resources or IT. The infrastructure phase is a time when nonprofits can think about evaluation systems that will meet their internal programmatic needs because the models themselves are stable enough to allow for meaningful measurement of quality and impact. Organizations might be growing and need to develop more hierarchical organizational structures.

The third and final phase is called "impact expansion"; in this phase, organizations have reached a certain level of capacity at both the program and infrastructure levels and now can focus proportionally more time and resources on external questions, such as: *How can the lessons we've learned be leveraged to benefit the field? Are there evaluation findings to share? Is our ED spending appropriate time* outside *the office, developing relationships with funders, advocating on behalf of the issues that are most important to our constituents, and otherwise engaging activities that somehow grow the field?* This phase is analogous to the maturity phase of the Stevens model. Both are aspirational, and both assume an upward trajectory. Figure 1.3 brings the TCC and Stevens models together.

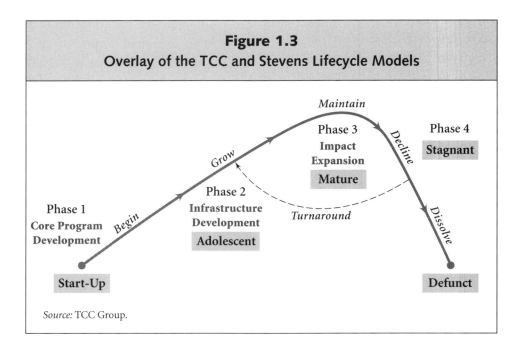

Figure 1.3
Overlay of the TCC and Stevens Lifecycle Models

Maintain

Phase 3
Impact
Expansion

Mature

Grow

Phase 4

Stagnant

Decline

Phase 2
Infrastructure
Development

Adolescent

Phase 1
Core Program
Development

Begin

Turnaround

Dissolve

Start-Up

Defunct

Source: TCC Group.

To help nonprofits assess and increase their organizational capacity, TCC Group developed the Core Capacity Assessment Tool (CCAT), an online organizational self-assessment that is taken by staff and board leaders of an organization to rate a number of indicators of organizational effectiveness. The CCAT measures capacity in four areas, assesses organizational culture, and places the organization at a phase on the lifecycle pyramid, based on how stakeholders rate the organization.[3] We will refer to certain CCAT scores and lifecycle placements at different points in this book.

The TCC model does address certain shortcomings in the Stevens model, but leaves other important questions unanswered, particularly those related to decline, turnaround, and dissolution. How does an organization get to these phases? Inattention to core program issues is certainly part of the equation, but there are other factors at play. Are there ways to predict (and thus prevent) decline?

John Brothers: The High-Arc/Low-Arc Model

In his earlier work with nonprofits, John found that although his clients understood the lifecycle, many of them—particularly those whose organizations were on the downward side of the curve—felt that the model did not adequately describe their trajectories. He started to notice a pattern among many of them, particularly those that had been on rapid growth trajectories (growth defined as significant expansion of programs provided, people served, sites established, operating budget, and so on): organizations that had a rapid growth pattern often experienced a similarly rapid decline. These he came to think of as "high arc." Low-arc organizations, in contrast, are those that are more cautious or deliberate in their growth trajectories and tend to both build and decline at similar rates. John started to believe that the rate of growth can define a nonprofit's future, *depending on the level of investment and attention the organization had given to lifecycle development.* Figures 1.4 and 1.5 illustrate the trajectories of high-arc and low-arc organizations, respectively.

An organization that attempts to do too much, too fast, can be positioning itself for an almost certain decline that will occur about as quickly as its growth and development. John developed the high-arc/low-arc model as a way to help nonprofits in decline understand how the rate of growth may have contributed to their difficulties.

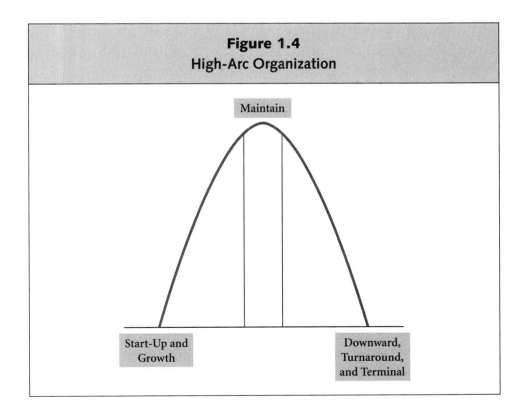

Figure 1.4
High-Arc Organization

Maintain

Start-Up and Growth

Downward, Turnaround, and Terminal

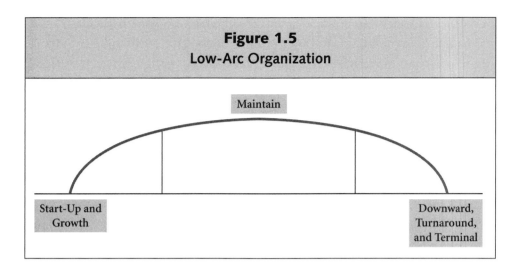

Figure 1.5
Low-Arc Organization

Maintain

Start-Up and
Growth

Downward,
Turnaround,
and Terminal

OUR PERSPECTIVE

As we stated at the beginning of this chapter, we believe that change is important and in fact essential. We chose to use the lifecycle because it is inherently dynamic—it assumes that organizations are, by definition, always evolving. Think of the scene from *Annie Hall* when Alvy is trying to break up with Annie on the plane back from California. He turns to her and says, "A relationship, I think, is like a shark. You know? It has to constantly move forward or it dies. And I think what we got on our hands is a dead shark."

Annie and Alvy's relationship died because it stopped moving forward. There is a certain parallel with nonprofits. The dying nonprofit, one might argue, is the one that simply cannot adapt and change in the ways it needs to, or doesn't understand the imperative to change until it is too late. Or it may be the organization that grew too quickly, without adequate attention to building its core program and infrastructure.

This question of arc becomes even more significant if we stop to think about the increasing importance of growth in the discourse on the role and purpose of the nonprofit sector in our society and think seriously about scale and what it means. There will always be problems in our society; identifying the means of taking successful programs to scale may be the way to address some of those problems more efficiently and effectively.

At the same time, there are many good reasons for nonprofits *not* to seek significant growth (even before the Great Recession changed the way many of us in the sector think about growth and sustainability). Some nonprofits, such as neighborhood associations, may have missions that are not consistent with growth. Others believe that "small is beautiful" and that the impact of their work will suffer if they grow beyond a certain critical point. Nonetheless, much of the thinking and investment related to nonprofit development has relied, to a greater or lesser extent, on assumptions about the inherent desirability of growth.

It is our hope that this book is relevant both to the organization that seeks to increase its reach as well as to the one that is deliberate in its decision not to expand. Both kinds of organizations must be conscious of the decisions they make with respect to growth, and both must be purposeful in how they plan to advance from one phase of the lifecycle to the next.

WHAT'S IN THIS BOOK?

The purpose of this book is to *help nonprofits become stronger by approaching lifecycle advancement as a type of change management* and to help leaders in the nonprofit sector figure out how to effectively shepherd a change process in their organization. Our intention is to provide a resource that

- Makes the case for a deliberate change process yet also acknowledges the very real challenges inherent in such efforts
- Normalizes and contextualizes the struggles that nonprofit leaders face
- Offers success stories
- Offers frameworks and tools that leaders can apply in their own organizations

Chapters Two through Six examine the five lifecycle phases, including a discussion of how an organization in decline can navigate a turnaround. Chapter Seven concludes the book with a summary of the key concepts and their application. Throughout the book, we draw on each of the three frameworks presented in this chapter, giving varying weight to one or another model, depending on the phase. What we have attempted to do with this book is articulate some of our assumptions about what is behind a successful nonprofit.

Back to Basics: "What Is Core"

This chapter will focus on the basics of nonprofit development. Both the start-up and the more seasoned organization may share similar first phases of the nonprofit lifecycle. One of the shortcomings of the Stevens model is that it speaks less well to the experience and needs of an organization that is years beyond being a true start-up, yet has some fundamental issues to address. Too often in the nonprofit sector, growth in size is emphasized over growth in impact and quality. The TCC Group model addresses this question through its lifecycle pyramid, complementing the start-up phase of the Stevens model with the concept of core program. The organization that falls into this phase of the lifecycle can be any age or size, but in all likelihood has to develop or revisit such fundamentals as mission, vision, and program strategy. Recognizing that core program organizations can be a heterogeneous group, this chapter discusses both the start-up and the seasoned organization that is going "back to basics."

DEFINING THE "CORE" IN CORE PROGRAM

For the core program organization, the organization's mission, vision, values, and program strategy are almost equivalent to its raison d'être. Here we offer a brief overview of these four elements; later sections go into more detail.

In order to incorporate as a 501(c)(3), a nonprofit needs a mission statement. Mission statements are most effective when they are concise and reflect the specific change or impact that the new organization seeks to effect. Strategy—the means by which this particular organization will go about achieving its mission—can be part of the mission statement, for it is often the strategy that differentiates a nonprofit from its competitors. The decision to include mention of strategy is up to the individual nonprofit, as long as the statement itself is short and sweet and focuses more on ends (the change) than on means (the strategy).

Organizational vision can be tricky for a nonprofit to define; this is especially true for the start-up. For many social entrepreneurs, the vision is a societal one—the type of world the organization hopes to create (for example, a society without violence, a community without homelessness, a region that embraces classical music and its symphony orchestra). There is nothing wrong with having a societal vision. Too many nonprofits, however, fail to lay out a clear vision for the future of their organization. It is easy to see why this would be the case for the start-up, which is by definition more focused on the bigger picture. And that may be OK, for a little while. Start-ups have enough to worry about in the first year or two to establish the other aspects of their core program strategy. But if they want to move beyond this initial phase eventually, they will be well served by establishing a statement that outlines a vision for the organization that will provide adequate support to its programs.

Third is the values statement, a collection of the core principles and beliefs that stakeholders agree must underlie every activity in the organization. An organization's values should be understood and shared by everyone in the organization, regardless of his or her title or role. They are the standards to which all internal stakeholders (for example, staff, board, and volunteers) agree to hold themselves accountable; they tend to endure over time. Words or phrases that commonly characterize a values statement include *respect for all, dignity, innovation,* and *excellence.*

Finally, we come to core program strategy, the way in which the organization achieves its mission. Core program strategy is about defining and implementing a coherent set of programs tied to a set of outcomes that support mission. The start-up organization is, generally speaking, most concerned with "launching" its core program. By definition, this is the work of the founder and the people with whom she surrounds herself. Initially, this may just be the board members, who very often are members of the community or personal friends of the founder, although there may also be a small paid staff. Salaries tend to be low; energy and passion tend to be high. Leadership in the start-up organization relies very heavily on a single founder or a core group of founders. In many cases, the board will be small and often a "working board," due to the lack of staff.

For the more established organization in core program phase, the salient issues related to program strategy are often about reassessing the programs themselves. For example:

- Do all our programs clearly relate to our mission? Are there any instances of "mission creep"? If so, what are we going to do about it?

- Are we clear on the results we seek to achieve through our programs? If so, do they support our mission? Do they make sense, given what we're good at and what our market demands? Are we clear on what our market demands?

Before we delve more deeply into these topics, we will spend some time discussing how an established organization might know it's in the core program phase. Whereas it's pretty clear to see how a start-up falls into this phase, most "seasoned" organizations wouldn't place themselves here; they almost always perceive themselves as much further up the curve or pyramid.

THE ESTABLISHED ORGANIZATION IN CORE PROGRAM: CHARACTERISTICS AND TELLTALE SIGNS

Remember that there is not necessarily a relationship between an organization's age and its lifecycle phase. It is not always a question of seniority or tenure. There are plenty of nonprofits that have been in existence for ten, twenty, even more than a hundred years, yet need to get back to the fundamentals of what it takes to run an effective, high-impact organization making a positive difference in the community.

This is a tricky and often sensitive discussion. There are many nonprofits that belong in this first phase, but by no stretch of the imagination could they be considered start-ups. Their programs are well established. Their board members are less likely to be friends of the founder; much of the time, in fact, the founder is no longer even associated with the organization. These nonprofits are well known in their communities or fields, yet their mission statements may be outdated or unclear. Stakeholders may believe that the mission statement is relevant, but an objective outsider might observe that the mission is so broad that any number of programs could (and often do) fit within it, leading to a set of activities that is less a coherent strategy and more a mixed bag of offerings. The organization lacks a compelling vision articulating where it is headed over the next several years, and program strategy may lack clarity or coherence.

Signs That Your Seasoned Organization Might Be in Core Program

1. Your mission statement is long and rambling, and either doesn't address impact at all or emphasizes strategy at the expense of impact.

2. You don't have an organizational vision statement—a clear and compelling description of your organization several years in the future—or the one you have doesn't align with your organizational priorities.

3. Your values statement is either weak, nonexistent, or inconsistent with management practices.

4. Your program strategy is not strategic. That is to say, it doesn't meet all of these criteria: firmly linked to mission, clear on results, and maximizing your core competencies and your "market niche."

TO PUT A STAKE IN THE GROUND, YOU NEED A GOOD MISSION

The mission statement is the articulation of what, at the end of the day, a nonprofit seeks to achieve in the world. On balance, it should be more about results and less about strategy. What is the difference you are trying to achieve through your work? For far too long, the sector has tended to reverse the order. Consider the two statements of purpose and which is the more compelling:

1. Anne's House provides home visiting and counseling services to all families in Midwood with children under the age of six.

2. John's Place promotes the physical, mental, and social health of all Midwood children under the age of six so that they enter school ready to learn and succeed throughout their educational careers.

We'd go with B. Although these examples are somewhat exaggerated, we hope that the main point comes across: that nonprofits are ultimately accountable to their stakeholders for achieving results, not providing programs.

As a rule of thumb, try to keep your mission statement to no more than two sentences (and those sentences should not be unduly burdened by multiple clauses, phrases, and other grammatical loopholes). We know this seems arbitrary, and in some ways it is. However, it is our experience that the longer the mission statement, the less consensus there was among the group of people who wrote it in the first place. Peter Drucker famously wrote that a mission statement should fit on a T-shirt, and although that might be overly restrictive, we do appreciate the point about brevity. A verbose mission statement may be a symptom of any number of underlying issues, including competing priorities among the people in the room the day the mission statement was written or a lack of shared understanding about the organization's core purpose.

Now, having said that, we want to make clear that we are not against mission statements which include references to strategy or "means." In fact, we feel that the means are often the differentiator for nonprofits. We once worked with a nonprofit on a new mission statement as part of a larger strategic planning process. The executive director (ED) looked at the pithy and outcomes-focused mission statement that would fit on the tiniest of T-shirts and gave the following assessment: "I hate it. This makes us sound like any other arts organization in this neighborhood." We had to admit that she had a point. This mission statement was nothing if not succinct, and its impact was stated unequivocally, but it also felt cold and generic. With our client, we worked on it some more to add information about what was distinctive and special about the organization. As long as you can stay within a two-sentence limit and keep the primary focus on results, go for it!

AN ORGANIZATIONAL VISION AS YOUR GUIDE TO SUCCESS

For the core program organization, the vision statement can be a powerful tool to integrate mission and strategy and also to consider the management issues that become increasingly important as the organization begins to near the infrastructure phase of the lifecycle. The vision we speak of here is the shared picture of where the organization is headed, typically three to five years in the future. (Some organizations, often those whose vision represents a dramatic difference from where they currently are, choose to have a ten-year vision statement. We do not have a strong opinion on this, as long as the organization's current decisions, priorities, and allocation of resources are closely aligned with the vision.) Too many nonprofits lack such a statement.

As an anonymous wise person once said, "We are limited, not by our abilities, but by our vision." Vision statements that describe a future state of an organization are actually an essential precondition for an organization's ability to advance through the lifecycle. They give stakeholders something to aspire to, while at the same time keeping everyone grounded in reality. A vision statement should articulate a future worth investing in, and it must take into consideration what is possible, as defined by human resources, financial constraints, conditions in the operating environment, and so on. For the seasoned organization, a new vision statement can be a great way to launch a process of revitalization and change.

Dan S. Cohen, in his book *The Heart of Change Field Guide,* talks about the critical role of the vision statement in an effective change management process. Change is by definition part of the lifecycle, which is dynamic and is always focused on some kind of improvement, growth, or adaptive process. Cohen states, "An organization might recognize that change is necessary and take steps to implement it, but without a clear vision, the change initiative will be direction-less and will likely stray from its intended path. It will also lack propulsion, the energy to keep moving forward."[1]

If your organization already has a vision statement, the following are some questions you and your team might want to consider when thinking about whether it's in good working order:

- Can all internal stakeholders, staff and board, talk in similar terms about where the organization is headed?

- Are organizational priorities for the next few years clear? Is there a common definition of success?

- Is the vision statement both aspirational and feasible? That is, does the picture of the future do a good job of balancing the big picture with the reality of where you are today? Is it reasonable to believe that you "can get there from here"?

- Is it compelling? Does it paint a picture of an organization that is vibrant and dynamic and that embodies excellence? Think of the colleague or associate you most respect. Is this vision statement going to make him wish he could serve on your board?

The vision statement should cover program strategy, but can encompass other aspects of the operations, such as staffing, leadership, or external communications. It really depends on what the organization's specific needs are. Core program organizations often need to consider management issues. For the established organization that is in the core program stage, management may, ironically, be too much of a focus; think, for example, of an organization you know of that has become more invested in its systems and sustaining the status quo, and less driven by mission, program quality, and impact. It may run reasonably efficiently, but it is probably not delivering programs that could be considered effective across the board, and it is almost certainly not doing work that would be considered innovative or dynamic.

For the start-up, management tends not to be the primary focus. Founder, board members, and any paid staff or other volunteers who might be in the picture are understandably consumed with the business of launching programs and getting the organization off the ground. For the start-up, the vision really is about the world that its founder and her team hope to achieve. It can be difficult to narrow the focus from the macro to the micro, or at least difficult to do so in a deliberate way. Not all start-ups are ready for a vision statement because they are more focused (and rightly so) on the program they are building. A vision statement might be more appropriate later on, when programs are better established. That said, we have worked with start-ups that have benefited from deliberately thinking about sustainability from the get-go. For these leaders, a simple vision statement outlining the basic tenets of success can be a helpful touchstone as the organization progresses.

VALUES MATTER

Although values statements—the articulation of fundamental beliefs and philosophy—are found in both the for-profit and nonprofit sectors, it is easy to see how the values statement might lend itself naturally to a nonprofit organization. If nothing else, ours is a sector that is driven by a desire to achieve principles or goals that the free market cannot or will not support, left to its own devices. Most people who work for a nonprofit organization do so because it allows them to have a job that matches their values. We are not saying that the for-profit sector lacks values or people who seek to live their values in their work—not at all. What we are saying is that the nonprofit workforce tends to be populated by people who seek jobs that will allow them to live their values.

Values statements are important for any nonprofit organization, regardless of lifecycle stage, and are a critical aspect of individual and organizational identity. We introduce the topic in this chapter because it has special relevance for the core program organization, both start-up and seasoned. If you are a start-up, a values statement can help shape your nascent organizational identity. For the seasoned core program organization, a values statement can help bring into sharper focus core principles that haven't been discussed for a while, or, perhaps even more exciting, can help stakeholders articulate the organization they are trying to rebuild or re-create.

Values for the Start-Up

For the start-up, values deserve consideration for a couple of reasons. First of all, it's too easy to take them for granted. One might argue that the start-up organization is all about values, but this is not necessarily the case. In fact, it is easy to overlook values given all the other things that a founder and her team need to focus on. And this is totally understandable. There is a hierarchy of needs in any organization, and articulating values may not be at the top of the list. Frankly, it may be too soon to be able to fully understand your organization's values if you are knee-deep in the process of developing programs and building a culture. So while maybe it's overkill to suggest an annual convening of key stakeholders to articulate values, we do recommend that, at a minimum, the founder remain cognizant of values that are driving the work—not just the mission, which is the reason for doing the work in the first place, but the principles and philosophies that influence the way in which the mission is carried out.

This last point relates to the second reason why it's important to be deliberate in articulating values from the early days. By being explicit, you put your cards on the table, thus allowing interested parties to understand more fully who you are and what you are building. And you create a forum for discussing and even debating these values as programs mature and the organization grows.

Values for the Established Nonprofit

For the seasoned core program nonprofit, a good values statement provides the important common denominator that can be the basis of positive growth and change. For this organization, which tends to be less focused on creating and more focused on doing, the trick is putting into place a process that is appropriately inclusive yet doesn't take forever. (As a side note, inertia is often what bogs down the seasoned core program organization.) If the organization is in the midst of some kind of capacity building effort, such as strategic planning or a rebranding, the forum for a values discussion already exists. If not, then it becomes the role of the leader to find a way to make it happen, perhaps by working it into a staff or board retreat or by assembling an ad hoc work group.

Let Your Values Be Your Guide

The importance of a good values statement was demonstrated to us during a planning retreat for a large human services agency that was facing significant financial concerns. The organization offered a variety of programs to low-income people, and most of these were funded almost entirely through government contracts. There was one program, however, a reentry program for men who had recently been released from prison, that relied almost entirely on the agency's very limited unrestricted funds. This program was widely regarded within the agency as very high quality. During the planning retreat, a discussion on strengthening the organization's financial position eventually turned to possible program cutbacks, and the reentry program was one of the first candidates. There was an uproar in the room, with stark divisions between those who liked the program but could not make the business case for it, and those who felt that serving this particular part of the population, which is so neglected and marginalized, was a moral obligation and that the organization needed to do everything in its power to retain this program. A clearly articulated, well-understood values statement might have set the stage for a less divisive debate.

Values statements are useful tools to help nonprofits shape, understand, or re-create their organizational identities. In their book *Switch: How to Change When Change Is Hard,* Chip Heath and Dan Heath provide a framework for helping individuals become willing agents of change. Key to their model is the importance of motivation—finding levers that will encourage and facilitate new behaviors. One powerful lever is a newly adopted or cultivated identity, one that represents the type of change that is sought and embodies a specific aspiration or goal (for example, conservationist, professional). These authors point out that identities aren't limited to individuals; organizations can assume them as well. When an organization defines the right identity, it shapes how it sees itself in relation to its mission, its work, and the challenges it faces in the world. "Identity is going to play a role in nearly every change situation."[2]

How does a nonprofit successfully establish its values? There are two steps: first, define and articulate them; second, live them.

Step One: Define and Articulate Your Values

It is a good idea to bring together a group of key stakeholders, both staff and board, to identify those core principles or philosophies that underlie your work no matter what. *What are those standards to which we are going to hold ourselves accountable? What can our clients or customers expect from staff interactions, no matter what the circumstances? What sets us apart from others who do similar work?* These are all questions that are part of a rigorous values discussion.

Try not to overprocess. Values statements are definitely a case of less being more. With too many items, a statement can quickly turn into a laundry list, and the individual components become less meaningful.

As is true of the mission conversation, it is a good idea to reexamine values periodically, say every few years, if only to collectively affirm that this particular set of core values continues to accurately portray those beliefs that are most important to the organization. In fact, we think there's a compelling case to be made to consider mission, organizational vision, and values as three separate components of an overarching definition of organizational identity. If mission tells us why we exist and organizational vision is what we aspire to be, then the values are really the how, in terms of guiding philosophy and approach.

Convene a representative group of staff and board members. (It's OK to have the entire staff and board participate if the organization is small.) Try to enlist someone who is a good facilitator and can keep a conversation moving. For some, it's helpful to hire an external consultant with expertise in nonprofit organization development. For others, a consultant is not a viable option, for any number of reasons. In such cases, we recommend the following:

1. Do *not* have the ED facilitate. It is too easy to succumb to the temptation to lead the witnesses, and anyway, the ED should be involved in shaping the dialogue.

2. If the facilitator is a board member, be careful that it be someone who can be objective, can elicit and encourage various points of view, and has the skills needed to synthesize input. Many boards are lucky to have such individuals as members, but not all. (*Note:* Sometimes a former board member can be an excellent resource for jobs such as this one.)

3. If you need to look outside the organization but cannot pay a consultant, consider asking a trusted colleague from an organization with a similar mission.

A discussion about values can be an important and productive way to engage a representative group of stakeholders in a conversation about the core principles that everyone in the organization, staff or volunteer, must agree to uphold. Having said that, in general we recommend that the group stay small, say eight to twelve participants. For a start-up with few or no paid staff, a small group may be the only option. For a larger organization, this number may feel artificially small. There is no magic number; just keep in mind: the larger the group, the more skilled the facilitation and the more structured the conversation will need to be In the large-group scenario, it may not be possible to leave the meeting with a well-defined, "fully baked" values statement. In such cases, the group can arrive at a list of values that, if not perfect, is at least better defined than what they started with. Then it is the job of the ED, perhaps working in consultation with a small group of advisers, to shape the list of principles into an eloquent vision statement that complements the mission statement and expresses what is vital about the organization.

The following is a sample values statement, that of the Foundation for Louisiana, formerly the Louisiana Disaster Recovery Foundation (LDRF). The Foundation for Louisiana was founded by Governor Kathleen Babineaux Blanco as an independent foundation on September 5, 2005, six days after Hurricane Katrina struck the Gulf Coast region of the United States. Since its inception, the Foundation for Louisiana has made grants to further Louisiana's recovery process in three areas of programmatic focus: housing, small business, and community engagement. The board and staff developed this values statement as part of a larger strategic planning process.

Sample Values Statement: Foundation for Louisiana

The board and staff of the Foundation for Louisiana are guided by the following set of core values and beliefs:

- Increased access to resources and opportunity strengthens vulnerable communities and improves the quality of life for all residents.
- Achieving equity and inclusion for all Louisianans requires effective policy and systemic change.
- Growing economic opportunity spurs innovation and creates shared prosperity.

- The grassroots wisdom of Louisiana residents is one of our most valuable resources.
- Given appropriate resources and support, communities are able to solve their own problems.
- Individuals and families have the right to maintain their dignity amidst disaster.
- Transparency and accountability are cornerstones of integrity and institutional success.
- Collaboration and continuous learning improve the reach and quality of our work.
- A diverse board and staff, representative of the diversity of our state, provide the best leadership for the Foundation.
- Informed and engaged leadership is essential to the sustainability of both the Foundation and its work.

Step Two: Be Sure to Live Your Values

This point cannot be overstated: it is far worse to have a values statement that is not honored than it is not to have a values statement in the first place. To disregard the principles that an organization's leaders have publicly espoused will only result in cynicism and disappointment on the part of staff. It is, in essence, a betrayal of all stakeholders but especially staff, one that will damage morale.

Although this observation might sound abundantly obvious, the reality is that we have heard countless stories from nonprofit staff members about leaders whose behavior flies in the face of their organization's stated values. For example, the board of a youth-serving organization we once worked with abruptly closed down its much-beloved rural recreation program that relied heavily on unrestricted funds, in response to an imminent budget crisis. The decision did significant damage to the morale of the employees and participating families, who had great affection for the program and what it represented to the organizational identity—a respite for children living in low-income urban communities. In the end, the decision may have been the right one for a whole host of reasons, but it was the sudden nature of the decision and lack of clear communication with staff and families that felt to them like a disregard of the values that made the camp such a cherished part of the organization.

BE SURE YOUR STRATEGY IS . . . STRATEGIC

So far, we have talked in this chapter about mission, vision, and values, but not program strategy, the fourth piece of the core program puzzle. For many (perhaps most) core program organizations, their strategy is not especially strategic, meaning that it is not well aligned with long-term goals and objectives and does not maximize internal capacity and expertise. The separate components do not fit together seamlessly in a way that is mutually reinforcing; the whole is not greater than the sum of the parts.

Asking Questions

In her book *Seven Turning Points: Leading Through Pivotal Transitions in Organizational Life,* Susan Gross describes an organization that, in the absence of strong priorities, has become "fragmented and parochial" and has "fiefdoms" in competition rather than coordinated departments functioning as part of an integrated whole.[3] Strategy is perhaps the toughest criterion to address, both conceptually and in practice. It is one thing to develop an organizational vision or rewrite a mission statement (notwithstanding the dozens of clients we have had over the years who would sooner walk over hot coals than attempt to rewrite their organization's mission statement). It is quite another to look critically at all of your organization's programs and services and ask the following set of questions:

- Do the various programs and services your nonprofit offers align with your mission statement and reinforce your vision statement?

- Do all of your programs support a shared set of longer-term results in a meaningful way?

- How do you make decisions about which programs to implement? To what degree are the decisions based on the following criteria:

    1. What do we know we do well or can we learn to do well in reasonably short order?

    2. What are our desired outcomes as an organization, and will this new program or service support them?

    3. Is this decision being driven primarily by available funding?

It may go without saying, perhaps, but we'll say it anyway: we strongly believe that questions 1 and 2 are the preferred criteria to use when making decisions about what programs to add, grow, or eliminate. But finances are an essential part of the decision-making process, and certainly we would never recommend that a nonprofit pursue programs that align with mission and have clear results but lack a sustainable funding stream. Furthermore, we recognize that few, if any, nonprofits operate under ideal circumstances. Many do adopt programs because of a newly available funding stream, and too many are forced to reduce or eliminate programs because revenues have dried up. For us, the question is really this: on balance, how do decisions get made? If questions 1, 2, and 3 were represented on a pie chart, how large would each piece be? Which factors drive decision making?

Using a Logic Model to Clarify Your Strategy

The logic model is a tool that is helpful for developing, implementing, and refining a strategy that is in fact strategic. Born of program evaluation methodology, the logic model is a visual way for stakeholders to establish a clear and logical path between their desired social impact (often articulated as the mission statement), outcomes leading to social impact, and program strategy in ways that are thoughtful and grounded in the most recent knowledge of effective practice and that balance aspirational goals with results that are feasible. A logic model template is illustrated in Figure 2.1. (In Chapter Three, we will be looking in more detail at the logic model of the nonprofit New York Cares.)

Working from "right to left," the logic model exercise requires stakeholders to begin with the end in mind: the change they hope to effect in the world. For many nonprofits, this desired change is quite broad (for example, eliminating poverty, promoting democratic societies, or preserving the environment), and ends up being articulated as a mission statement one could drive a truck through. And even for an organization with a more tightly focused mission statement, the reality is that the social impact that any given nonprofit is trying to achieve is going to be on a larger scale than what can be accomplished within a few years or even decades. The logic model exercise asks stakeholders to break down their mission or statement of social impact into more manageable, achievable results called "outcomes," those specific results that a given nonprofit can expect to achieve, or at least make a meaningful contribution toward achieving. These outcomes—short term, interim, and long term—establish logical connections between social impact (mission) and strategy.

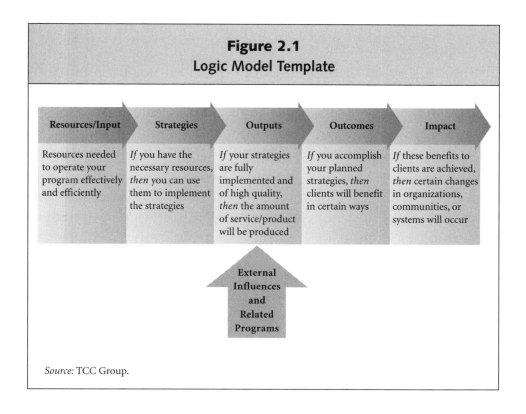

Figure 2.1
Logic Model Template

Resources/Input	Strategies	Outputs	Outcomes	Impact
Resources needed to operate your program effectively and efficiently	*If* you have the necessary resources, *then* you can use them to implement the strategies	*If* your strategies are fully implemented and of high quality, *then* the amount of service/product will be produced	*If* you accomplish your planned strategies, *then* clients will benefit in certain ways	*If* these benefits to clients are achieved, *then* certain changes in organizations, communities, or systems will occur

External Influences and Related Programs

Source: TCC Group.

It is imperative that outcomes represent change—whether it's in an individual's knowledge or behavior, a society's attitudes on a particular issue, or in a more enlightened public policy. The number of performances in a given season or of brochures distributed at a health fair are not outcomes; they are outputs. An output is not a demonstration of change; it is merely documentation that someone did what she said she was going to do. (This is not to say that outputs are unimportant but simply to point out that they should not be confused with outcomes.)

You may be wondering what a tool most often associated with evaluation has to do with the lifecycle. The answer is simple: no matter where an organization is in its lifecycle, it must always ensure that its core program is solid. This is a basic tenet of the TCC Group pyramid: core program is the foundation of any strong organization. A good logic model is useful for sorting out core program issues for several reasons:

1. It keeps mission at the forefront, and links it with strategy by articulating a rigorous set of outcomes that serve as a bridge between the difference the

organization hopes to make in the world (social impact) and the way in which it goes about doing it (strategy).

2. The logic model requires that strategy be laid out clearly and succinctly. Multimillion-dollar agencies manage to adequately communicate their strategies in a short space. There is a certain discipline in this, demanding that each word be chosen carefully.

3. Logic models also challenge stakeholders to take a hard look at their existing strategy and think carefully about those parts of it that do not easily support desired outcomes. This, in turn, can lead to important conversations about whether those strategies that support desired outcomes should be expanded and others be phased out.

4. It lays out the underlying assumptions that are critical to both understanding and refining a strategy. If strategy is the what and outcomes are the why, assumptions begin to speak to the how. *What forces are most influential in our ability to deliver successfully on our strategy? What helps; what hurts? What are the premises that undergird the whole enterprise?* When well defined, underlying assumptions provide important contextual information that helps paint the bigger picture.

FOUNDER'S SYNDROME . . . NOT JUST FOR FOUNDERS ANYMORE

For the organization that is moving toward the infrastructure phase, the evolving role of leadership is an essential issue. *Founder's syndrome* is a phenomenon that can afflict a nonprofit led by a founder whose sense of ownership in the organization is so great that objectivity is compromised; the founder's perceptions of the nonprofit and its needs may overrule the opinions of others and may not always be in the organization's best interests.

Much has been written about founder's syndrome, which may be the start-up organization's greatest challenge. (The term even has its own Wikipedia entry.) When we use the term, we are referring to an organization whose identity, ideas, and culture are so reliant on the founder that effective leadership on the part of others on the staff and board is inhibited. Founder's syndrome is certainly a real phenomenon, but we actually think that it occurs in many nonprofits that are *not* start-ups—namely, those that have been led by the same executive director

(ED) for ten years or longer (basically long enough so that no one actively affiliated with the organization can really recall the achievements or contributions of the ED before the current one) and those whose identity is closely tied, both internally and externally, to that of the ED.

Founder's syndrome, in most cases, is not the same as total denial or lack of awareness of the organization and its needs. Certainly, there are plenty of start-ups whose founders are willing to invest in enhancements, such as appropriate IT, HR policies, or a better facility. There are plenty of start-ups that grow their operations to match programmatic need. The big risk for an organization in the start-up phase arises when the founder has sole or primary ownership of the core program (mission, vision, and strategy) and is unwilling or unable to share ownership. It is not uncommon for the founder to hire program managers who will not challenge his vision for the organization or tamper with the program strategy. It is also very common to see boards that are lulled into complacency due to their trust in or devotion to the founder. The board may grow in size, but not in its ability to lead the organization.

An organization might grow under this scenario, but absent a leader who is able to share ownership of the core program, potential for increased impact will be limited. The energy is still centered around the founder, and it may be that no one is ready to act any differently.

Because this problem is by definition about leadership, it stands to reason that the solution lies there as well. Someone, or some group of individuals, must be able to put the needs of the organization before those of the individual leader. Mission must have primacy. It is the job of the ED to execute the mission; however, protecting and defending the mission of the organization is perhaps the board's most important function. Founder's syndrome, it could be argued, is what you get when one or both of these parties fail to adequately perform in this most fundamental area.

The paradox here is that founders are, presumably, about nothing if not their organization's mission. How can it be argued that founder's syndrome is the result of an inability to make mission the top priority? Assuming for the moment that the current mission is the right one for the organization, we think the answer lies in understanding that a mission may be constant, but its implementation needs to change over time. Let's recall our definition: founder's syndrome occurs when ownership is the sole property of one or a few at the top. A corollary to that might be that the so-called owners are unable to adapt or modify the way that the mission is implemented. Our knowledge of the lifecycle tells us that as needs and challenges change over time, so too do the solutions, and if the founder or longtime leader cannot or will not adapt, problems will arise.

Pete York, the director of research and learning at TCC Group, has analyzed an extensive dataset of hundreds of nonprofits nationwide that have completed the CCAT. Findings from his analysis point to the importance of adaptive capacity: the ability to monitor, assess, respond to, and stimulate internal and external changes. York's analysis shows that effective leaders are individuals (or teams) who can adapt effectively to changes either within their organization or outside it. For example, an organization's programmatic growth may demand that the ED give managers additional decision-making authority. The adaptive leader will interpret this "datum" and begin to work out a plan to address it, demonstrating adaptive capacity. The resistant leader might insist that no additional funds should be "taken" from programs to support infrastructure, or may be reluctant to share decision-making power. Another example: an American symphony orchestra in a rapidly changing, increasingly diverse community finds its ticket sales dropping. The adaptive leader might reach out to leaders of emerging ethnic communities to understand how to make the orchestra's offerings more relevant, and begin to modify the schedule to reflect other cultural traditions. The resistant leader might say, "Our schedule is a faithful representation of the tried-and-true Western classical canon. People still come to hear Beethoven's *Fifth* or Handel's *Messiah*. We're sticking to the basics."

Generally speaking, the ability to adapt depends in large part on the leader and his or her capacity for self-awareness. Change Management 101: the leader has to perceive a problem before embarking on a journey to solve it. It is often difficult to be self-critical in a productive way, though, when one is consumed by the endless litany of demands that come from leading an organization. This can be especially true for the founder, but certainly leaders of established organizations can experience this as well. The relatively recent introduction of executive coaching into the nonprofit sector has great potential here. After all, the role of the nonprofit leader is never easy, regardless of the organization's lifecycle stage. Even though the job is exciting and rewarding, it can also be lonely and at times grueling. It's easy to see how any leader might lose perspective, and a good coach (or a trusted peer or a sage board member) can play an invaluable role by helping the leader look in the mirror and be honest about the reflection. Such a scenario assumes two preconditions: (1) the existence of trust, which we discuss further in the next section, and (2) the ability to communicate effectively. These elements tend to go hand in hand; it is hard to imagine effective communication between the ED and staff, or between the ED and board, in the absence of trust. The leader has to be able to trust his or her adviser; the adviser has to be able to help frame things in a useful way.

This level of self-awareness really demands a lot of a nonprofit leader. Think of the fairy tale "Snow White"; the story probably would not have become a timeless classic had the Wicked Queen not freaked out when the mirror reported that she was no longer the fairest in the land. It is not uncommon to meet founders who are unable or unwilling to acknowledge the need to lead or manage differently. In such cases, trust and communication are insufficient because the founder cannot conceive of implementing the mission in any way that is different from the way he or she has done it. In other words, for this leader, there is only one vision for the organization, and it is the property of the founder.

"Holding up the mirror" in this case can be a much dicier proposition, and not only because of a lack of self-awareness. The conventional wisdom about start-up boards is that they are populated by friends of the founder. An organization with a more mature board can see when it's time to ask the founding mothers and fathers to make room for new leadership or to broaden the bench of leaders. But the resistant leader will keep friends and other "loyal supporters" on his board, to the extent that they do not challenge his decisions and priorities. Not surprisingly, the staff members who tend to succeed under such leaders are those who do not argue for a different management model or for otherwise changing the status quo.

TAKING IT TO THE NEXT LEVEL: THE IMPORTANCE OF TRUST

A related discussion, one that is important for all organizations but especially those in the core program phase, concerns trust. Any constructive conversation about significant change is going to depend, to a greater or lesser extent, on the degree of trust that exists within the organization—the trust between the ED and board, the ED and other staff, the organization and its funders. They have to trust that the uncharted waters they are about to sail will get them to a better place than the one they are currently in. They have to trust that the people steering the ship are up to the task. And they have to trust that the inevitable disagreements or differing perspectives are healthy and are ways in which new models of operation will be created as the organization moves to the next phase of development.

This is asking a lot of any nonprofit team, but can present special complications for the start-up. Many nonprofits are very tight-knit operations, with a small staff and board collaborating closely, led by their founder. Many such organizations, accustomed to the excitement of the unpredictable first few years of operation, are characterized by nothing if not by trust. Organizational identity might be based at least in part on an "us against the world" mentality that provides resilience during particularly challenging times. What happens, though, when someone in the organization suggests that it is time to consider paying staff a higher salary, that systems are needed to manage staff more fairly or consistently, or that program staff should be managed by someone other than the ED? Such conversations can be threatening to an organizational leader because by saying that it's time for a new approach, they imply that the current approach is no longer working or is not working sufficiently. A system that was seemingly in equilibrium only hours before is suddenly revealed to be unstable.

Resolution of such situations can be a tricky business. Much is at stake, and complicating matters further is the shifting balance of power that is occurring within the organization. The vision of the ED, heretofore the law of the land, is now being called into question by either board or staff members. Technically speaking, the board supervises the ED, but oftentimes, the board has delegated authority to the founder. When the board is suddenly asked to exercise its power, everyone can be thrown into a tailspin.

It is at moments such as these that trust among the stakeholders in an organization becomes critical. Let us be clear in how we define the term, because too often, trust is synonymous with harmony or agreement. Trust does not mean always sharing a similar point of view—in fact, trust means being able to remain engaged in a constructive way when conflicts arise. For the core program organization, which, you will recall, is typically struggling to define the foundational elements of mission, vision, values, and core program strategy, lack of trust can be a tremendous barrier to progress. This often becomes apparent through the tension that arises when an organization is trying to get to the next phase or when a new vision emerges that will change the organization's identity.

Organizational change can be successful if trust and values intersect in the right way. Think about it: for an organization moving from core program to infrastructure, what is going to be most reassuring to people and best help them manage the inevitable instability? The answer is the values that stakeholders share and the trust that individuals have that these values will endure, regardless of the change that will take place. In 1999, Peter Drucker and Pete Senge, two great thinkers on the subject of organizational transformation, discussed leadership and change. During this conversation, Senge observed that "Nature preserves a small set of essential features and thereby allows everything else to change." Making an analogy to organizations, Drucker hypothesized that the "essential feature" in organizations is trust in the "values . . . not tools. That is the way you help create trust. And on that basis you can have very rapid change and it doesn't upset people."[4]

BoardSource, the nation's leading voice on nonprofit governance, speaks to this from the perspective of the board-ED relationship in its very useful publication *The Source: Twelve Principles of Governance That Power Exceptional Boards.* The first principle: "Exceptional boards govern in constructive partnership with the chief executive, recognizing that the effectiveness of the board and chief executive are interdependent. They build this partnership through trust, candor, respect, and honest communication."[5] BoardSource staff will tell you that this first principle is first among equals—that is, although all twelve are important, in the absence of a strong board-ED partnership, it is impossible to develop and sustain the other eleven core principles.

Drucker, of course, was talking about organizational change in a general sense, not thinking about the specific application of his theory to, say, a start-up going through growing pains or a fifty-year-old nonprofit struggling to move into the infrastructure phase. We would suggest that values and trust are necessary to effectively managing a change process in a nonprofit organization, regardless of the stage of development. For a core program organization, especially one that actively aspires toward advancing to the next phase of the lifecycle, it is our firm belief that establishing values and trust is a fundamental component of healthy development, one that will support longer-term organizational effectiveness.

An Exceptional Start-Up

Sadie Nash Leadership Project was incorporated in September 2001 with a mission of promoting leadership and activism among young women, a purpose it fulfills through increasing the participation of women in social, political, and economic decision making. Sadie Nash works primarily with young women of color from low-income communities in New York City and Newark, New Jersey.

The Sadie Nash philosophy is laid out clearly on its Web site, as are the core tenets of the program model:[6]

> Sadie Nash is designed to guide young women through a process in which they come to understand the importance of their individual life experiences, and how these experiences can be applied to taking action and making change. Our philosophy, which is our guiding force, is built on the following beliefs:
>
> - that the foundation of leadership lies in service and activism
> - that positive reform will result from challenging accepted notions of leadership
> - and that young women can be a catalyst for social change.

Sadie Nash Leadership Project

Sadie Nash is a fascinating case study on many levels. First, it remains a small organization, with an annual operating budget of approximately $600,000, although it has grown rapidly in its first decade. With relatively few resources, Sadie Nash gets a lot done. It has excelled in virtually all areas of organization development: mission clarity, program strategy (including consistent measurement of quality and outcomes), management, staff and volunteer leadership, financial management, and external communications. Sadie Nash has performed at such a high level, in fact, that in 2010 it was awarded the Gold Prize for Overall Management Excellence by the New York Times Company Nonprofit Excellence Awards program.[7]

Thinking about this organization, I (Anne) felt that it had a lot to share with regard to all phases of the lifecycle. I chose to highlight Sadie Nash in start-up, however, because of the very interesting lessons to be derived about how leadership really laid the foundation for later success.

Please tell me a little bit about your approach to leadership. The organization is going on ten years old, and the founder, you, remain at the helm, yet you seem to have avoided many of the pitfalls of founder's syndrome.

I had always worked in nonprofits. I first worked as a social worker. I was then running a very successful arts fellowship program, and I found that I was experiencing a crisis of spirit. I am a very political person and a feminist. At the time, I was a single mom of an adolescent girl and had worked as a volunteer in domestic violence. I wanted to work with women and asked myself, *What am I doing? I'm doing a great job as an ED, but I'm missing my heart.* So I took a risk and resigned. I took five months off to think about what would come next. In creating Sadie Nash, I veered radically off my path, but I was also doing what I was passionate about. And it fit my skill set that I'd acquired from previous jobs. I did enter with a skill set. Many founders don't have it; in that way I might be unusual. I knew far less about programs, but that's why I hired a program director right away.

In terms of my approach to leadership, a big part of my job is to make sure that staff is happy and the organization is fiscally sound. I endeavor to inspire the team by encouraging them to think about the big picture. We have a philosophy of "diagonal growth," meaning that we want to always be increasing both the number of girls we reach *and* the effectiveness of our programs. We apply this to all parts of the organization, including staff. We are clear with staff that we want them to grow as individuals in their jobs, and also to grow as leaders in the organization. We are deliberate in investing in our people and their professional development and have a strong history of promoting from within, including hiring program participants.

We have used a shared leadership model from the start. I manifest that in a variety of ways. I assembled the board quickly and got their input on mission. We decided on the name and then wrote the mission. I had a vision for the programmatic components I was interested in—feminism, women, social justice, education. I enlisted an early board member to help me put my thoughts into writing, an organized narrative. And we went from there.

The program model we started with was preliminary and rather skeletal. This was early on, the first summer. We focused on academic rigor, the importance of role models, and active leadership. I wanted much more than simply providing trainings. And those pillars continue to be the driving forces in our program today. When the first program director started in January 2002, we decided to run a summer program, and then the voices of young women started playing a part. That's where management and mission started to coexist—we started listening to the opinion of our participants, so that *agency* as a concept is not just in program and mission, but also in management.

The first program director started running focus groups, and we learned that the girls wanted to hang around and do something during the year. Not all of our programs are driven by girls, but their voice has always been present. They are on the board or are at our retreat, or we're reading their evaluations. They are an important driving force.

We have always had a pretty strong board; this is a big theme for us. The board has cochairs, and functions overall as a really strong team. That was my backbone, and you have to trust in that. It's a really strong working relationship—their leadership and mine. I didn't put myself on the board, because I really wanted opportunities for other voices at the table. Reflect, process, bring people to the table.

I have a strong belief that values have a big role to play in an organization's ability to ascend up the lifecycle. Can you talk a little bit about the role that Sadie Nash's values have played in shaping the organization?

This is how I define values: as tone. It's incredibly important to me that there be a tone that has value. An organization that is highly professional—"tight." And I wanted people to feel happy. Sounds Pollyanna, but it's really true. I'd worked at a lot of places where the staff is not happy. Very nuanced, how to make staff happy. Not just being a relaxed boss. At the time, I couldn't define what that meant, but now I see that a lot of it is fairness. If people work overtime, you need to compensate them. It's important to appreciate people. There has to be a sensitivity. So it's no surprise we have high staff retention. It was also important to me that we be regarded as highly professional by the outside world—return calls, run fair staff searches, don't tokenize youth, etcetera.

We feel the need to continually move forward, and people associated with Sadie Nash would say that it is always exciting. We are pretty active. It might mean that we're rethinking something or exploring something. I don't want to be bored. If I'm bored, others will be too. We try to maintain a sense of exploration, innovation, excitement.

Diversity is a big value, too. I'm not an idiot; I recognized that I'm a white woman and that I don't "represent" Sadie Nash participants with regard to race and ethnicity. I knew this was a weak point. We are deliberate in our efforts to hire people of color at all levels of staff, and have a racially diverse board. Program participants are represented on the board as well and are recruited to join the staff.

Leaving Core Program

The Christian Activity Center (CAC) is a faith-based organization, affiliated with the Southern Baptist Convention, that serves young people ages six to eighteen living in East St. Louis, Illinois. With a focus on education, health, and recreation, CAC serves children and youth from 3:30 to 8:00 every day during the school year, and full days during the summer. It has maintained its presence in its current location since the 1950s, although programs have evolved over the decades.

Like many faith-based organizations, CAC is an intensely mission- and values-driven institution. Its current ED is the Reverend Chet Cantrell, who came to CAC as a missionary in the early 1980s.

When considering the story of CAC, it is important to understand the extraordinary assistance it has received through a four-year capacity building grant from the Deaconess Foundation in St. Louis, Missouri, as part of the first round of the Deaconess Impact Partnership (DIP), a comprehensive investment in the capacity of select nonprofits serving children and families in the St. Louis metro area. All told, the grant brought hundreds of thousands of dollars into CAC, in both direct and in-kind contributions. Clearly, the DIP grant made possible a level of growth that CAC probably would not have otherwise achieved; Cantrell would be the first to agree with this observation. But even with this major "leg up," I strongly believe that CAC is a good model of a seasoned organization that transcended the core program phase. There are plenty of organizations that have received major cash infusions and weren't able to handle the pressure that comes with growth. CAC did, I believe, because it was already strong in core program in important ways and was willing to learn in those areas where it was weak.

Can you talk about the point at which you think the organization really began its process of transformation?

Early on, when I'd been here a year or so and really tried to assess needs in this community and then find people to sell a vision to. When key people bought that, it started a transformation for us, and from that we were able to start posturing ourselves. We got some significant corporate help. UBS helped us build the gym and that helped us programmatically; we could collect data and talk about what works. Then we started adding people with good program experience. From there, we began to look for ways to fund staff and tried to get foundation buy-in to jump-start things.

Programmatically I was there because I brought with me some tools from past experience. I knew what to expect and knew basic things about what would help kids. I was strong on program. We needed to put structure around our ability to do mission. That took a long time and really served as a springboard to where we are today.

Over the years, the mission has not changed; the basic vision has been the same. Our transformation really began when I realized that if we invested in infrastructure, it would sustain us long term. We'd always been hand to mouth. I'd begun to see that what I was doing was not serving us in terms of sustaining the mission. I couldn't sustain the people, which is the absolutely essential element for program. I knew that diversifying funds was really about building relationships with people.

It is clear that the mission and values of CAC have been steady over time, while program strategy has evolved. Can you talk a little bit about how you engaged stakeholders in creating a strong, cohesive model that could serve as the foundation for the organization's success?

We tried to have as much staff buy-in as possible, from the beginning. We revisited the mission and got the staff involved in creating the vision. We went back to scratch on the roots of why we do what we do, and how it can best be done, asking what skills do we need. We started trying to hire more strategically and wrote more detailed job descriptions while keeping our culture intact. There was some natural attrition, but we kept those people with certain skills that we could elevate and benefit from. We also realized that we needed a structure where not everyone is under the ED. We are getting better all the time and bringing people along.

In terms of the program, I've always wanted to help parents, but a mentor taught me that I can't. What I have to do is raise the next generation, and we stay focused on the kids. You can get lost in trying to change lifestyles or invest everything in bringing up the generations. We have kids who are very successful at parenting. Adults who came here as kids, and I learn stuff from their parenting. I really do. Kids who come from broken homes have created homes that are not broken. People are engaged with their kids at school, read to their kids as babies, talk about books and education.

Building on that, what is truly at the "core" of CAC?

Intentionally loving kids. Being intentional about what it means to love a kid. We are very values driven. Attitudes, demeanor, things you can do that help kids. It's holistic. But you have to be intentional about the kind of relationship you build with the kid. I indoctrinate my staff in a philosophy of how to deal with kids. This is what kids need: they need to know that they are loved, accepted, and welcomed here. They don't want a best friend in an adult. If you're intentional about the messages you give to kids and create cultures for them. We want them to know the value of playing and how to play together. The value of education. The mantra of "12 plus 2"—that their ability to have numerous life options depends on graduating from high school and having two years beyond that. Often they aren't getting it anywhere else. What are they saying to us about their dreams? I tell staff, you have to say these things, or else they aren't going to know. Word choices, expectations, and knowing why. You have to pour meaning into it all the time—here is why, this is what helps.

We try to ask ourselves what really will help kids over the long haul. We know from the huge amounts of research that supervised kids, growing up in a holistic environment that has expectations of them, will do better than those who don't. You need to present them with options that mean something. In our town 60 percent of kids drop out of school. Mentally they drop out by the third grade. We're trying to give kids a love of learning that is infused throughout all the departments. Being at grade level in the third grade is an important benchmark, and we need to maintain that level of achievement through the sixth grade. If we can keep them engaged through the eighth grade, chances are good that they will carry that to the tenth grade. And if they make it to tenth grade with a C+ or better, there's a 98 percent chance of graduating high school. This is a message that permeates everything we do, and we make sure that this focus on education is balanced with the recreation and physical play they need.

How has your own leadership played a role in the organization's evolution?

I try to be open to everything, including the scrutiny that comes with evaluation, which is scary. I knew some of it, but also I learned some new things. Right now, I'm trying to wrap my head around how to best do the people part. I'm an introvert by nature, and I'm at a point where I have to find a way that I can serve the mission in a nonprogrammatic kind of role. I've done everything that my staff are doing, and I could jump right in. Not jumping in—that was my heartbeat. I had a little struggle with my heart for a while. I'm happy to talk to people. It's easy to say thank you. It's much easier for me now.

CCAT Findings: Core Program

A review of the 360 organizations in TCC Group's CCAT database that were in the core program lifecycle stage found that, on average, organizations were strongest in the following areas (strength defined here as a score of 220 or above out of 300):

Adaptive

Environmental learning: using collaboration and networking with community leaders and funders to learn about what's

(continued)

going on in the community and stay current with what is going on in the field.

Leadership

Leader vision: organizational leaders apply a mission-centered, focused, and inclusive approach to making decisions, as well as inspiring and motivating people to act upon them.

Challenges included the following (challenge being defined as a score of 190 or less out of 300):

Adaptive

Organizational learning: self-assessing, using assessment data or findings to conduct strategic planning, and following through on strategic plans

Organizational resource sustainability: maintaining financial stability in order to adapt to changing environments

Programmatic learning: assessing the needs of clients and using program evaluation as a learning tool

Program resource adaptability: easily adapting to changes in program resources, including funding and staff

Leadership

Leadership sustainability: cultivating organizational leaders, avoiding an overreliance on one leader, and planning for leadership transition (including having a succession plan)

Board leadership: board functioning with respect to empowerment through connecting people with the mission and vision of the organization, holding organizational leaders accountable for progress toward achieving the mission and vision, conducting community outreach to educate and garner resources, and meeting regularly and providing fiscal oversight

Management

Conveying the unique value of staff: providing positive feedback, rewards, and time for reflection

Supporting staff resource needs: providing the technical resources, tools, systems, and people needed to carry out the work

Technical

Technology skills: ability to run efficient operations

Program evaluation skills: ability to design and implement an effective evaluation

Outreach skills: ability to do outreach, organizing, and efficacy

Marketing skills: ability to communicate effectively with internal and external stakeholders

Fundraising skills: ability to develop the necessary resources for efficient operations, including the management of donor relations

Facility management skills: ability to operate an efficient facility

Facilities: the proper facilities (space, equipment, amenities, and so forth) to run efficient operations

Organizational Culture

Unifying: engendering open and honest communication across all levels in the organization, leading to a sense of a cohesive "group identity"

Reenergizing: supporting time for staff to reflect on their work, socialize, and reconnect with why they are doing the work

Source: TCC Group.

Infrastructure/ Adolescence

As a nonprofit solidifies the foundation of mission, vision, values, and program strategy, other organizational needs become more urgent. Infrastructure, the second phase in the TCC framework, is the stage at which more emphasis needs to be placed on building infrastructure. This can include a more hierarchical organizational structure, better-defined HR systems, increased financial controls, and more complex financial management systems. The organization's leaders, both board and staff, must recognize the need for more sophisticated management tools and processes and then identify the resources that are needed. In addition, leaders must redefine their roles to meet the organization's changing needs. This is the time for leaders to think longer term and clarify the type of "institution" they aim to build.

It is not for nothing that in the Stevens lifecycle framework, the infrastructure phase is referred to as adolescence. This phase is full of change and is often stressful. It is both exciting and awkward. For the organization leaving the start-up phase, infrastructure can be thought of as a critical turning point, a crossroads where the organization's leaders consider long-term sustainability and what kinds of systems and leadership need to be in place. For the established organization, it might be about strengthening the systems that are already in place. It may require an acknowledgment, tacit or explicit, that too little has been invested in infrastructure to date and that great programs need well-run organizations.

What does an organization that is in the infrastructure/adolescence phase look like? In his book *Navigating the Organizational Lifecycle: A Capacity Building Guide for Nonprofit Leaders,* Paul Connolly describes the typical adolescent phase as entailing "expansion of new programs, broader outreach, more staff and larger quarters. Frequently, the adolescent nonprofit experiences instability when it does not adequately anticipate the systems required to support this growth."[1] There is a core truth to this description; many of us have been part of a young nonprofit that has "outgrown" its current capacity. Programs may be oversubscribed; the lack of systems is a chronic source of stress and an impediment to getting the job done. This can indeed lead to instability. In this chapter, however, we want to look closely at the concept of instability and apply it somewhat more broadly. Such systems as IT, financial management, or HR management matter, of course, but we believe that the concept of instability is pivotal to the infrastructure phase because of the deep change that is inherent during this phase of organization development. The infrastructure organization is one that has a basic clarity and consensus on mission, vision, values, and program strategy, and is ready to rethink the type of organization it wants or needs to be.

Whether this phase is called adolescence or infrastructure, much of the thinking about it is, understandably, focused on growth. Although this focus on physical or material expansion makes intuitive sense, especially when thinking about the start-up, we suggest that such a view is incomplete. Although the adolescence phase is in many respects about program growth, adding systems, and becoming more sophisticated, we feel that even more relevant to this discussion is another, more profound aspect of development: creating a more fully formed identity—defining the organization that you wish to become and determining how best to get there. In *Seven Turning Points: Leading Through Pivotal Transitions in Organizational Life,* Susan Gross characterizes this as "the need for infrastructure," noting that "The culture of the organization must shift so that the staff and board as well as the executive director place much more value on institution building and management."[2]

In terms of the high-arc/low-arc model, the organization that is in this phase is clearly on a growth trajectory. A key challenge for the infrastructure/adolescent organization is defining the type and rate of growth that are most appropriate. The sector is rife with examples of organizations that have grown for growth's sake, perhaps convinced that organizations that don't grow will stagnate. Or perhaps an organization's leaders have been more opportunistic than strategic in seizing growth opportunities. It is quite common, for example, for a nonprofit to pursue funding opportunities that do not align well with its mission or the results the organization has committed to achieving.

There is no single appropriate rate of growth for the nonprofit in the infrastructure/adolescence phase. If an organization is too cautious, it may miss important opportunities for funding or collaborative partnerships. If the nonprofit is growing in a reckless or unstructured way, or growing beyond its capacity, growth will most likely be unsustainable. These challenges apply to both programmatic growth and organizational growth. For example, we once worked with a small advocacy organization that received a sizable grant to build its infrastructure to better support its programs. Enhancements included IT upgrades, a bigger office space, and addition of staff to focus on development and external communications, and all were made in a short period of time. Program staff resented the significant infusion of funds into administration, and over time it became clear that the organization lacked the management capacity to integrate these enhancements effectively and sustain them. This started a spiral of internal dissension that resulted in nearly all staff leaving the organization, either quitting or being asked to leave. The organization was not able to regain its footing, and after two very difficult years, it closed its doors.

Was the high rate of growth this organization's fundamental problem? Probably not. But the overly rapid and ultimately misguided growth did put pressures on the organization that it could not handle. Growth that was more measured and strategic might have actually helped address the leadership and management challenges. It was on a high-arc trajectory when it should have pursued a low-arc path.

The most common trap, we have found, is growing either in the wrong direction (for example, adopting mission-inappropriate programs) or too fast (for example, adding programs without paying enough attention to needs related to administration, management, leadership, or operations). We will spend time in this chapter talking about a few critical aspects of nonprofit organizations that warrant special attention during the infrastructure phase. As we share the lessons we've learned, we hope that at least one point is clear: the growth that occurs in infrastructure will set up the organization for success (which we discuss in Chapter Four) or serious difficulties (discussed in Chapters Five and Six).

PLANNING FOR ORGANIZATIONAL GROWTH

If the core program phase is about establishing the foundation, infrastructure is about continuing to build the organization through the expansion of programs, administration, operations, or a combination of these. Planning for growth in a smart way involves clarifying the type of growth, the rate of growth, and the strategy for achieving it. When we work with organizations in the infrastructure phase that are considering some sort of expansion, we take them through a set of critical questions. Here we've grouped the questions in terms of programs, management and infrastructure, and sustainability.

Programs

The following are questions that any nonprofit leader should ask before engaging in expansion of programs.

1. Do we want to expand existing programs, or add new ones? If so, why?

2. How will expanding our programs help increase our impact?

3. Do we have data that support the expansion of current programs or the addition of new ones?

4. How does this expansion relate to our existing program strategy? Does it build on core competencies we already possess or reinforce the outcomes we've committed to achieving? Should the model be revisited?

How might an organization go about answering these questions? Question 1 is about gaining clarity on the rationale or motivations behind program expansion. Is expansion driven by funding opportunities? Has the competition stopped offering a particular program, providing an opportunity to expand? Have demographic shifts created new needs or an increase in demand? Stakeholders should try to be as clear as possible in identifying the various stimuli behind a potential expansion.

Questions 2 and 4 can best be answered by going back to the logic model. Recall that the logic model is a graphic depiction of how the organization links mission impact to desired outcomes to strategies. Certainly, the logic model would be a useful resource for answering question 2, validating that the proposed programs do in fact link to the types of results you are seeking to achieve, and question 4, looking at new potential programs in relation to the existing strategy.

Question 3 is in effect another type of validation. This question challenges stakeholders to justify expansion of programs by documenting the success of existing programs. *Do we have data that support us in doing more of the same programs? Can we add programs on the basis of what the latest research has to say about the most effective models or promising practices?* In other words, whenever possible, expand programs on the basis of available data, whether they're collected internally through your own evaluation efforts or available externally, based on research in your field.

Let's use New York Cares as a hypothetical example. New York Cares is New York City's largest volunteer organization, running volunteer programs for twelve hundred nonprofits, city agencies, and public schools. The organization works with partner nonprofits to identify their most pressing needs; creates projects to bridge the gaps; and recruits, trains, and deploys teams of volunteers to make a difference. New York Cares also invests significant resources in the recruitment, training, and support of its volunteers, as well as in field-building activities, such as conducting research and providing technical assistance to peer organizations. The logic model for New York Cares is illustrated in Figure 3.1.

Suppose that New York Cares is presented with an opportunity to expand a program, such as a customer service initiative that will add services and supports to those already offered to the partner agencies. Let's walk through the questions posed here and think about some of the possible considerations for the organization.

1. *Do we seek to expand our programs? Do we want to expand existing programs, or add new ones? If so, why?* The program enhancements would represent a new initiative for New York Cares; this wouldn't strictly be an expansion of existing programs. The organization's leaders would have to articulate some of the motivators for adding this program. They might have determined that their partner agencies have demand for such a service; there may be a donor interested in supporting New York Cares in expanding in this area.

2. *How will expanding our programs help increase our impact?* Looking at the logic model, there is a case to be made that there is a link between offering new services to partners and the desire of New York Cares to make New York a stronger and more vibrant community and a better place to live. That is a fairly broad statement of impact, though, and might not be a sensitive enough

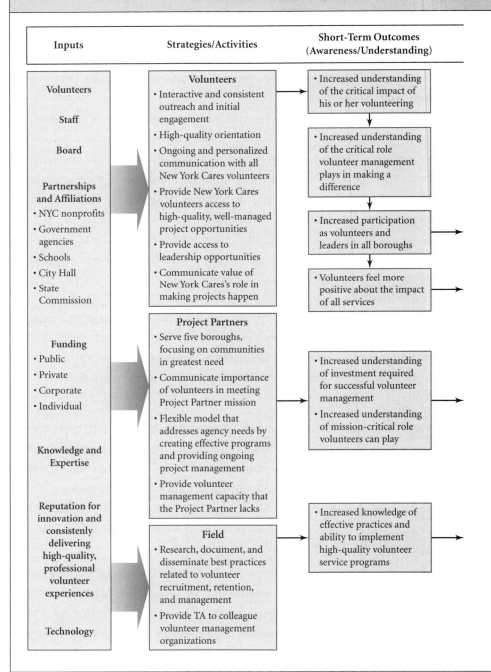

Figure 3.1
New York Cares Logic Model

Inputs	Strategies/Activities	Short-Term Outcomes (Awareness/Understanding)

Inputs

Volunteers

Staff

Board

Partnerships and Affiliations
• NYC nonprofits
• Government agencies
• Schools
• City Hall
• State Commission

Funding
• Public
• Private
• Corporate
• Individual

Knowledge and Expertise

Reputation for innovation and consistenly delivering high-quality, professional volunteer experiences

Technology

Volunteers
• Interactive and consistent outreach and initial engagement
• High-quality orientation
• Ongoing and personalized communication with all New York Cares volunteers
• Provide New York Cares volunteers access to high-quality, well-managed project opportunities
• Provide access to leadership opportunities
• Communicate value of New York Cares's role in making projects happen

Project Partners
• Serve five boroughs, focusing on communities in greatest need
• Communicate importance of volunteers in meeting Project Partner mission
• Flexible model that addresses agency needs by creating effective programs and providing ongoing project management
• Provide volunteer management capacity that the Project Partner lacks

Field
• Research, document, and disseminate best practices related to volunteer recruitment, retention, and management
• Provide TA to colleague volunteer management organizations

Short-Term Outcomes (Awareness/Understanding)
• Increased understanding of the critical impact of his or her volunteering
• Increased understanding of the critical role volunteer management plays in making a difference
• Increased participation as volunteers and leaders in all boroughs
• Volunteers feel more positive about the impact of all services

• Increased understanding of investment required for successful volunteer management
• Increased understanding of mission-critical role volunteers can play

• Increased knowledge of effective practices and ability to implement high-quality volunteer service programs

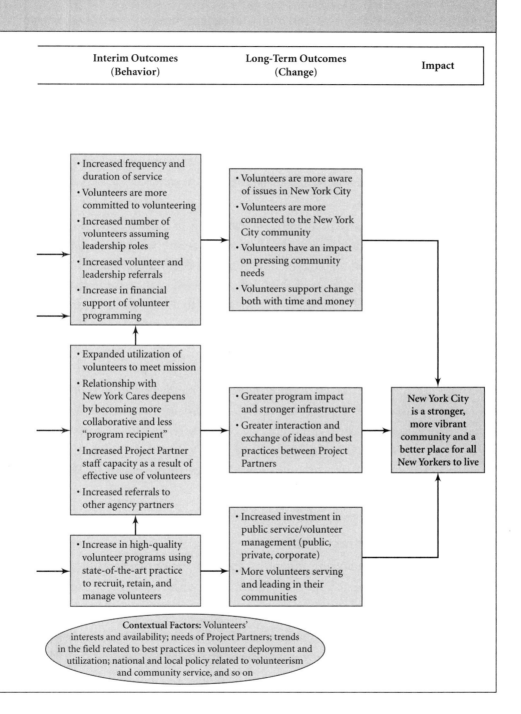

Interim Outcomes (Behavior)	Long-Term Outcomes (Change)	Impact

• Increased frequency and duration of service

• Volunteers are more committed to volunteering

• Increased number of volunteers assuming leadership roles

• Increased volunteer and leadership referrals

• Increase in financial support of volunteer programming

• Volunteers are more aware of issues in New York City

• Volunteers are more connected to the New York City community

• Volunteers have an impact on pressing community needs

• Volunteers support change both with time and money

• Expanded utilization of volunteers to meet mission

• Relationship with New York Cares deepens by becoming more collaborative and less "program recipient"

• Increased Project Partner staff capacity as a result of effective use of volunteers

• Increased referrals to other agency partners

• Greater program impact and stronger infrastructure

• Greater interaction and exchange of ideas and best practices between Project Partners

New York City is a stronger, more vibrant community and a better place for all New Yorkers to live

• Increase in high-quality volunteer programs using state-of-the-art practice to recruit, retain, and manage volunteers

• Increased investment in public service/volunteer management (public, private, corporate)

• More volunteers serving and leading in their communities

Contextual Factors: Volunteers' interests and availability; needs of Project Partners; trends in the field related to best practices in volunteer deployment and utilization; national and local policy related to volunteerism and community service, and so on screen to apply. Let's back up to long-term outcomes. This new area does seem to support the long-term outcomes of greater program impact and stronger infrastructure. How about at the short-term and interim outcomes levels, which are much closer to the actual work of the organization? The customer service initiative might reasonably hold up there as well, as it could conceivably support the following interim outcomes: expanded utilization of volunteers to meet mission; deepened relationship with New York Cares by becoming more collaborative and less "program recipient"; and increased project partner staff capacity as a result of effective use of volunteers. To fully answer the question, the organization's leaders would need to consider carefully the assumed relationship between this potential program and the extent to which it would support these outcomes.

3. *Do we have data that support the expansion of current programs or the addition of new ones?* The organization does not currently offer this program, so it would not have evaluation data documenting its effectiveness in this particular arena. There may be data from evaluations conducted with existing programs, or data may be available from other organizations that have experience in providing such services, or there may be research regarding promising practices in this area.

4. *How does this expansion relate to our existing program strategy? Does it build on core competencies we already possess or reinforce the outcomes we've committed to achieving? Should the model be revisited?* This would be a new initiative for New York Cares, although one certainly related to the core work of the organization. Leadership would need to carefully consider whether the effort involved in launching such a program would be worth the payoff to New York Cares, its volunteers, and its partner agencies.

Management and Infrastructure

In the spirit of "form following function," an organization needs to be run and managed in a way that best supports program quality. The following are questions we recommend our clients ask to determine which investments need to be made:

5. Where do we need to enhance the infrastructure in order to better support programs, either the existing programs or an expanded model?

6. What is the right sequencing of these activities and enhancements?

7. Will these enhancements involve hiring staff? If so, how can we best integrate the staff into our existing infrastructure? What skill sets (programmatic, administrative, managerial, and so on) will we need to add to our existing mix? How will the roles of existing staff change?

8. How might the job of our leaders change? Will the executive director (ED) be able to delegate certain responsibilities? Will this growth or expansion require that we call on the board to provide new types of expertise? (For example, if enhancements include a more sophisticated external communications function, do we have such expertise on the board?) How should other staff members' jobs shift in response?

In many respects, questions 5 through 8 are at the heart of the issues the infrastructure organization faces, all aimed at helping leaders envision and create the organization that is needed to support programs and mission. They are essentially strategic planning questions, but you do not need to engage in a strategic planning process to answer them. You might start with an organizational vision statement, discussed in Chapter Two. The organizational vision statement draws a picture of what the organization is going to look like at some future point in time. Although it is a key tool in a strategic planning process, a basic organizational vision can be created from a few thoughtful discussions on the part of the organization leaders, focused on what they want the organization to be known for and what investments will need to be made. Consider the following hypothetical organizational vision statement for New York Cares:

> New York Cares will be well-known and highly valued as New York City's leading volunteer organization, a leader in the field of volunteer management, and a provider of high-quality services to address critical social needs in the city. We will achieve this by increasing the capacity of the nonprofit sector through our core competencies of volunteer management and program delivery. To support this work, we will maintain a strong external communications function and make strategic investments that will result in more effective and efficient operations.

This statement makes clear what the organization is going to be known for and the areas in which it is "best in class." These core competencies are consistent with the strategies in the logic model. With regard to investment in the organization, we see that New York Cares has chosen to give high priority to external communications and strategic investments in operations. This does not mean that the organization won't invest in other areas, such as fundraising or professional development of staff, but rather provides a sense of its organizational priorities. This answers question 5, *Where do we need to enhance the infrastructure in order to better support programs, either the existing programs or an expanded model?*

Question 6 relates to sequencing of activities. The answer might depend on several variables, including available funding or the relative urgency of specific needs, such as IT upgrades or alleviating unsustainable workloads. Sometimes it's a question of finding the low-hanging fruit that will allow progress to be made quickly while developing a plan for implementing more complicated or expensive enhancements. For New York Cares, the staff probably needs to do some more work to determine what enhancements it needs to make in order to achieve the operational goal of efficiency and effectiveness and how to best prioritize those enhancements.

Questions 7 and 8 are growth questions and may not be relevant for all organizations. "Leveraging communications," for example, might translate into a more deliberate plan for using social media. It may be a responsibility that can be assumed by existing staff, using existing resources. In contrast, it might involve launching a major public engagement campaign focused on increasing voluntarism in the city. Not only would such an effort require significant resources of time and money, but it also would have the potential to redefine aspects of the organization's work. It might, for example, require expansion of the current communications department, or it might increase the public profile of the organization to such an extent that senior staff members find themselves redefining their roles.

Sustainability

Too often, organizations that find themselves in a position to grow either their programs or their infrastructure do so without fully thinking through whether the enhancement is sustainable. Sustainability is often thought of in terms of finances—the ability to cover the costs of a program, additional administrative staff, or larger office space—beyond the life of a grant. Sustainability is also a function of organizational culture and readiness, and should be considered in this light.

9. How can we ensure that these enhancements are financially sustainable? Do we understand the true costs to our organization? If these enhancements are

supported by grant funds, what is our plan for sustaining them once the grant has ended?

10. How will we share the plan for these enhancements with staff? How do they tie into our vision for the organization? Why are these particular enhancements needed at this point in time? How can we best support the staff members who will be responsible for implementation?

These final two questions speak to the challenges in maintaining enhancements once they have been implemented. If New York Cares adds new communications or program staff, what are the assumptions about how the organization will continue to support them over time? How will they be fully absorbed and integrated?

Last but certainly not least, question 10 is really at the heart of change management. All change, even the most positive, elicits a certain degree of stress. Stakeholders are being asked to adapt to something new, and this is almost always a challenge. Furthermore, resources are always limited, and choosing one option means forgoing others, which is almost certain to please some stakeholders while disappointing others. For the leaders of New York Cares, managing this tension might involve engaging staff in conversations about why the customer service initiative is the right investment now and in the future, or why an expansion of the communications function takes precedence over relieving overcrowding in the office. It is the job of leaders to implement a vision by allocating resources as effectively and efficiently as possible and providing stakeholders, such as staff, volunteers, and clients and participants, with a compelling rationale for the decisions.

Many of these management and operational issues facing the infrastructure/adolescent organization are covered well in other books, including those by Stevens and Connolly. In the next two sections, we chose to focus the discussion on two elements that we think are less well understood, or that at least receive less attention in discussions about capacity building. They are the evolving role of the board in the infrastructure organization and the critical importance of organizational culture in strengthening an emerging nonprofit.

THE ROLE OF THE BOARD

In the discussion on the core program phase, we focused primarily on the role of staff leadership, particularly that of the ED. In the infrastructure phase, as in every other lifecycle phase, the ED is essential, but we feel that the role of the board is not as well understood and deserves special attention. For some organizations, such as start-ups or those that are emerging from a crisis, the board has played a very active, hands-on role and must now allow staff to make decisions and lead. Or perhaps the board has played a rather passive role and now finds itself needing to catch up with the strides that staff have made. Either way, what we are talking about is the need for the board to evolve with the organization, ideally leading (as opposed to trailing or, worse yet, resisting).

We want to press the pause button here and note that this may be one of the most intractable problems we've encountered in our combined twenty-five-plus years of work with nonprofits. Successful board governance is clearly a challenge for the sector. We expect great leadership from people with little to no expertise in either the substance or mechanics of the organization they are running. It often seems that the current governance model, if implemented as stated, collectively requires the leadership of Winston Churchill, the cultural diversity of Sesame Street, the passion and commitment of Mother Teresa, the wealth of Bill Gates, and the emotional intelligence of Mr. Rogers. Then there is the question of supply and demand: there are approximately 1.5 million nonprofits in the United States, each of which needs to have a board with an average minimum of three members. Many boards are three to five times this size. It is probably safe to assume that at any given moment, thousands of nonprofit boards are recruiting new members.

Certainly there are many wonderful, high-functioning boards that add great value to the nonprofit organizations they serve. But there are many others that fall far short of the requirements of the job. Add to this the tremendous demand for board members and a limited supply, along with the inherent imbalance in the power dynamic between board and staff (as the ED works for the board), and you have a potentially volatile situation. On one side is the ED, who runs the organization and has, in most cases, unparalleled knowledge about the organiza-tion and its position. On the other side is the board, which is a group of volunteers who by and large spend relatively little time focused on the organization, may not have expertise in either the substance or operations of the organization, and yet whose job is to ensure that the mission is fulfilled, the public's trust is upheld, and the organization has the resources it needs to do its job effectively—and, of course, to oversee the ED.

It is a delicate relationship, to say the least. An ED may have considerable power, but at the end of the day it is the board of directors that is legally responsible for fulfilling the mission and upholding the public's trust. If the board does not feel that the ED is performing sufficiently, the board has the option—some might say the obligation—to terminate employment. When the "mutually respectful and trusting relationship" that BoardSource describes in *The Source* does not exist, there is the potential for all sorts of problems.[3] EDs might seek to shore up their own power base, and control the board to the extent possible. Or the board, fearing that the ED is "getting out too far ahead" of them, may micromanage the ED or undermine his or her efforts to implement meaningful change.

You might reasonably be wondering, *Does this tangent about the potential perils of the board-ED relationship belong in a book on lifecycles and change management? And why here, in a chapter about infrastructure?* The quality of the board-ED relationship can make or break an organization's ability to become stronger and reach its potential to fulfill mission, and is an important consideration at any phase of the lifecycle. Infrastructure/adolescence is about defining the organization that will carry out the work that was defined in the core program phase. The role of staff, in many respects, becomes increasingly clear as the organization develops systems, institutionalizes its programs, and, in some cases, professionalizes. The role of the board can be more challenging to define and execute successfully. For example, many boards struggle to fulfill their role of setting policy or to become more effective in raising funds on the organization's behalf. As the work becomes less concrete, it can be more difficult for the board to understand exactly how to add the most value.

As we've discussed in this chapter, the infrastructure phase is really about an organization fully defining and establishing its identity. Certainly the core program phase, with its focus on mission, vision, values, and program strategy, is the point at which the organization's central purpose is defined (or, in many cases, redefined). But infrastructure is the phase during which a nonprofit's leaders must decide what kind of organization is needed to maximize programmatic impact. We are all well acquainted with the familiar tensions related to investing in systems such as IT or human resources. Less straightforward, but just as critical, are understanding, managing, and ultimately accepting the shifting roles of board, staff, and ED. These shifts must occur if an organization is to become higher functioning and more fully realized.

So roles must shift as an organization evolves; that seems to make intuitive sense. But how does that happen in a relationship that is characterized by an imbalance of power, such as that between the board and the ED? That, we think, is one of the critical questions of the infrastructure phase, and it really has little to do with administration or systems. In fact, it is a critical leadership question. And although conventional wisdom on the infrastructure phase does, in fact, address leadership, it tends to do so in terms that are prescriptive—for example, the board must become more professional, or the board should shift from a management role to one that is more focused on policy and fundraising. Connolly describes a "deeper sense of organizational ownership. . . . [T]he board will need to relinquish its operational role and focus more on advice, oversight, and long-term planning."[4]

As anyone who has been an ED, served on a nonprofit board, or been a consultant to a board knows, this is all easier said than done. As a species, the nonprofit board is a pretty heterogeneous group. However, in our work, we have observed a few types of boards that we tend to see at the helm of an organization in the infrastructure phase.

The Weak Board

This is the board that simply does not lead, the one for which the phrase "rubber stamp" was coined. Quorum at meetings is never certain. The ED continually struggles to find people who will do work outside of board meetings. The board may overrely on the ED for direction and lack the ability to challenge ideas or initiatives that may require further deliberation or debate. Ideas for doing things differently or improving practices tend to disappear pretty quickly. This board may meet the minimum fiduciary requirements, but it also runs a real risk of scandal or other type of catastrophe because of the inability to effectively set policy, monitor progress on implementation of strategic goals, and hold the ED and itself accountable.

Many organizations that are "led" by the weak board do not make it out of the core program phase because leadership cannot clearly define the foundational elements of mission, vision, values, and program strategy. Those that do emerge from core program tend to do so because of the ED's talent, charisma, and passion, as well as that of the staff that he or she hires. This is an organization that succeeds despite its board, not because of it. Although many nonprofits that have a weak board do experience growth, there are limits to how far they will be able to progress. As an organization matures, the need for strong leadership only grows; staff, led by the ED, can take an organization only so far. Without a board that can complement or challenge the staff's vision, an organization won't be able to attract the breadth and depth of resources it needs to be truly effective.

The weak board is a real challenge for the infrastructure organization. The strong leader who helped the organization emerge from core program may become frustrated and pursue opportunities elsewhere. The board, unable to fully understand or acknowledge its role in creating the problem, may actually feel relieved by the ED's departure and seek to hire a leader who does not have as strong a vision as his or her predecessor.

The weak board can change, but doing so is a challenge. In our years of working with nonprofit clients, we have been struck by the power of inertia and just how difficult it can be for boards to improve. Even boards that have term limits and actually enforce them seem to have a culture that transcends turnover of its membership. In those cases where a board does become stronger, typically the board has decided that the status quo is not in the organization's best interests and must change. Perhaps not surprisingly, the catalyst for such change often occurs when there is a critical mass of new board members who can bring a fresh perspective to the board's traditional approach. Three new members seem to be a good number.

Recruiting a critical mass of new, highly qualified board members is never an easy task, and although it may be challenging to do so when the board is weak, it is certainly possible. Much has been written on board recruitment, so we won't spend too much time on that topic here. However, we will note that we see this opportunity to reinvigorate a flagging board as a particularly important one, especially for the infrastructure organization. The infrastructure phase is really the time during which nonprofit leaders are making critical decisions that will help define the organization's identity. This is the time when the organization is inventing—or reinventing—itself. Absent a board that can rise to the occasion or at least aspire to do so, the infrastructure organization will most likely miss a critical window of opportunity.

The Hijacked Board

A variation of the weak board, the hijacked board is one in which there exists a schism between the majority of board members and a vocal and powerful minority that feels very strongly about protecting the status quo or some other interest. Often this schism emerges as the result of a change effort initiated by the ED that is particularly threatening to a group of board members. It is easy to imagine how the infrastructure organization, implementing any number of changes, both large and small, suddenly finds itself being led by a hijacked board.

This is the board that finds its meetings consistently derailed by a small but loud faction whose chief skill appears to be diverting time and attention from the topic at hand.

We once worked with an organization, for example, that nearly fell apart because of the conflict between the ED and board that emerged during a critical transition of roles and responsibilities. This was an arts agency in a small community, and a peer organization had recently closed its doors, due in large part to financial weaknesses exacerbated by the recession. Our client survived, although at times its own sustainability was in question. As part of a larger effort to restabilize, the ED was taking on more of an assertive leadership role in an effort to bring program and management practices into line with what he believed was going to help strengthen the organization and increase its relevance in the community. The board, which was uneasy relinquishing control, initially resisted his change efforts. After a few very acrimonious months, a few board members were asked to step down, and relations between the ED and the board calmed down considerably. Yet as the ED continued to introduce new practices, such as implementing changes in the organization's financial management policies (which had been recommended by the external auditor), the treasurer, supported by the finance committee, rebelled and told the ED not to implement these changes because she feared (erroneously) that it would expose the organization to an unacceptable level of risk. This, in turn, undermined the authority of the ED and prevented the organization from receiving a clean audit.

Even though the majority of members frequently disagrees with the agenda that a rebellious faction seeks to advance, it is typically the case that the majority will remain silent and avoid confrontation. Often the board chair will not take them on either, perhaps reluctant to censure peers, either publicly or privately. Meanwhile, the ED becomes increasingly frustrated. A board is a group of peers that is responsible for its own conduct and decisions, and the ED is not one of these peers. Even if the ED is on the board, he or she is the employee of the board. The board must hold its troublesome members accountable for their behavior, but the ED, as an employee of the board, cannot and should not.

The alternatives are for the board chair to have a private discussion with the perpetrators and let them know why their behavior is destructive and that it needs to stop. This seems like the obvious answer, but it occurs so infrequently that we feel compelled to mention the other option: peer pressure from the board itself. We believe that the most effective way to end the "tyranny of the few" and, more broadly, to build an effective governing body is to build a board with a strong shared understanding of norms—a cohesive board. A cohesive board can work together effectively, and its members have a strong shared sense of mission.

The Evolving Board

This is the board that knows it must change in order to keep pace with the organization's needs. This isn't to say that it always knows precisely how, but there is a general acknowledgment that some old habits must give way to new practices and, most likely, new people who can implement them. There may or may not be a strong chair, but usually there is a general sense of cohesion and trust both within the board and between the board and the ED. Oftentimes, bringing on a small but critical mass of new board members can be a powerful catalyst for change, as these individuals are not weighed down by beliefs about how past experience might influence the future, allowing them to ask new questions, be willing to try new strategies, or otherwise disrupt the status quo in a productive way. Disagreement or anxiety about how to move forward may well exist, but it doesn't ultimately prevent meaningful progress from occurring.

Conventional wisdom suggests that there is a straightforward recipe for board development that allows such progress to occur in a linear way. There is a shared sense of the organization's strategic direction and priorities, and general consensus that the status quo is no longer acceptable. Either formally or informally, there is an assessment of what is needed and where the current board falls short. Goals are established, and an earnest governance committee leads the charge to recruit new members, clarify roles and responsibilities, and develop a process for implementation.

As most of us know, this scenario is rarely, if ever, the reality. We have worked with nonprofit boards that seek information or training that will help them grow in their capacity to serve the organization. Such a process might begin with an assessment that includes confidential interviews with senior staff and board leaders and an anonymous board survey. The overwhelming majority (if not the entire group of respondents) will report that one of the qualifications that is most needed is the ability of individual members to contribute or access individual or corporate gifts on the organization's behalf. Fast-forward a few weeks to the stage after assessment, where we are putting together the board development plan. We will often hear considerable resistance to the idea of setting "stretch" goals for board giving or for all members to actively tap into their own networks to recruit people who can give at a higher level. Even if the board eventually agrees to set ambitious goals, successful implementation can be challenging.

Change is hard, as we all know. But it is also entirely possible, given the right conditions. The following are some strategies we've seen help evolving boards move up along the curve and, in so doing, power their nonprofits toward greater success.

Make board composition a priority. It is well established that as an organization evolves and changes, so too does what it needs from its board members. Successfully identifying, recruiting, and integrating new members onto a board is a significant task requiring ongoing effort. Every board, regardless of its organization's life-cycle stage, should always be thinking about composition, even if the board is at maximum size and each person is a perfect fit for the organization. In the rare instances where this is the case, we would bet money that it's not going to last very long, and the board should at a minimum be thinking about its pipeline. We have heard it argued that the governance committee (also sometimes called the nominating committee) is the most important committee of the board, and we might agree with this. Although ideally the entire board should be involved in the recruitment of new members, "committees of the whole" are rarely effective. Moreover, important as the governance committee may be, the board still has many other jobs to do, and making one group responsible for board composition and functioning maximizes the chances that these critical functions receive the time and attention they need.

Focus on building and maintaining a constructive board-ED relationship. We return to the first principle of *The Source,* which we discussed in Chapter Two: "Exceptional boards govern in constructive partnership with the chief executive, recognizing that the effectiveness of the board and chief executive are interdependent. They build this partnership through trust, candor, respect, and honest communication."[5]

This first principle should always be a priority, no matter what lifecycle phase an organization is in; it is important to realize, though, that the relationship between the ED and board will necessarily evolve with the organization. The stresses of the infrastructure phase demand that the ED and board work together in a positive way so that their attention can be focused on leading the organization and not questioning one another's judgment or motives. An obvious example is the board that replaces the founder with an ED who brings a set of skills that will help usher the organization through the infrastructure/adolescence phase. Whether communicated implicitly or explicitly, the mandate for change will take up considerable room on the new ED's agenda. The first year (or longer) will be focused on the board and ED's defining and communicating expectations, assessing success in achieving these expectations, and developing a trusting relationship. It is hard to see how the ED can otherwise be truly successful in implementing a change agenda.

Consider engaging in a structured planning process that will help clarify the board's roles and responsibilities and define what needs to occur in order for the board to fulfill its roles and responsibilities as effectively as possible. When so much is at stake (and we believe that for the infrastructure board, the stakes are indeed high), it is worth the time and effort to do things right. Some boards may require no more than a simple assessment followed by a discussion of findings and development of an action plan. Other boards might wish to conduct a more structured process, perhaps engaging an outside consultant with expertise in nonprofit governance who can offer an objective opinion about the board and where it needs to focus efforts to improve. A third option is to engage in a strategic planning process, if the organization does not have an existing plan. A true strategic plan will almost certainly include board self-assessment and a plan for development that reflect the organization's fiscal needs.

For any of these planning processes, we recommend that the board consider how to build the aspects of group cohesion, a concept borrowed from Donelson R. Forsyth.[6]

1. Social cohesion: Is the board an attractive group to the types of members it seeks to attract?

2. Task cohesion: How well can the board focus on tasks? Is there a strong sense of teamwork? Do members generally believe that the board can and will do what it sets out to do?

3. Perceived cohesion: Does the board have a strong sense of belonging, both for individual board members and overall?

4. Emotional cohesion: How would the morale of this board be described? What is the tone of meetings and interactions?

ORGANIZATIONAL CULTURE

We want to spend a moment on an important aspect of nonprofit organization development and change management that we believe is underappreciated and misunderstood: organizational culture. Organizational culture is similar to the role of values in that it is important at every stage of the lifecycle, but we believe that culture has particular relevance at the infrastructure phase. Going back to the metaphor of adolescence, the infrastructure phase is in many ways an organization determining who it is and what it aspires to be. Organizational culture is central to an organization's identity. And as Gross notes, the point at which a nonprofit's leaders start grappling with issues related to creating an organization that is in it for the long haul is the point at which the culture needs to shift.[7]

Organizational culture is one of those things that is hard to describe but easy to recognize. There are two definitions that we have found useful. The first is a TCC Group adaptation of the definition in Edgar Schein's seminal work *Organizational Culture and Leadership*: a pattern of shared basic assumptions and beliefs developed over time through solving problems and managing challenges, both internal and external. Schein actually describes organizational culture using a three-pronged model that includes artifacts (the cues about a culture based on what one can see, such as the way people dress, the arrangement of offices, or the tone of the ED's memos to staff); espoused values, which Schein defines as "conscious strategies, goals, and philosophies," or the things that we say we believe in or aspire to; and basic assumptions and values, which are the unspoken aspects of the culture that may not be initially easy to articulate as defining the culture, but that inform decisions, behavior, and conversation.[8]

The second comes from Bolman and Deal, in their 1991 work, *Leadership and Management Effectiveness*. Bolman and Deal's definition is consistent with Schein's and somewhat more concrete: culture is the pattern of beliefs, values, practices, and artifacts that defines for its members who they are and how they are to do things.[9] What is interesting about this definition is the implied level of self-awareness. How do you understand the culture of your organization, and what steps are you taking to put your values into practice? How is culture deliberately created?

First and foremost, values need to be clearly articulated, as described in Chapter Two. But although values are necessary, they are not sufficient. When we think about the culture of the infrastructure organization, we typically think about the organization making the transition from being informal and loosely structured to being more formal and more highly structured; for start-ups, this makes a lot of sense. This trajectory fails to account for the seasoned organization that has rethought its core strategy and reexamined its mission, vision, and programs. For this organization, the question is, *What type of infrastructure will allow us to support realization of the mission, vision, and program strategy?* Oftentimes, the seasoned organization already has administrative services (for example, HR, finance, IT, and so on) and needs to assess whether current systems are sufficient or appropriate in relation to evolving programmatic needs.

As Bolman and Deal suggest, an organization must engage in some self-assessment to understand its current culture. This might involve comparing the stated values with the "lived" ones and looking to see if there are discrepancies between the two. For example, if your values statement professes that yours is an organization that values learning and reflection, yet staff are provided no time to discuss their work, or evaluation data are used solely for accountability rather than for learning, then your professed values are at odds with your lived values. If there are inconsistencies (and there probably are), spend some time asking why, and what can be done to address them.

A common example is the organization that includes "innovation" on its list of organizational values. Perhaps reflecting pressure from funders to develop new and innovative solutions to intractable problems, many nonprofits will describe their work as innovative. When pressed to define how the work is innovative, however, leaders will struggle to identify convincing examples, because, truth be told, their work is not innovative. It may be responsive to needs and may provide a service in the community that no one else is providing; it may be doing a really great job. But none of those qualities make the organization or its services innovative. At a minimum, this type of discrepancy between espoused values and practice reflects a lack of self-awareness, which often leads to internal tension and may damage credibility with external audiences. Coming to terms with this type of inconsistency can be difficult and requires a certain level of humility among an organization's leaders. Thinking about the organization as an adolescent, this is an example of a "growing pain."

This leads us to another critical point about organizational culture in the infrastructure organization. Recalling our earlier observation about organizational identity, leaders, especially the ED, must recognize that the growing pains accompanying adolescence are due in large part to fear—fear of the unknown and fear among staff and, oftentimes, board members—that the organization is adopting an identity that is inconsistent with the one they originally signed on to. It is critical that staff and board leaders balance change with consistency—that is, even though much is changing, there are certain "nonnegotiables" that will remain in place. For example, many nonprofits in the infrastructure phase find that they need to put in place systems, policies, or positions that will increase accountability. Such changes for the start-up might include job descriptions or, for the more seasoned organization, integrating performance measures into existing position descriptions or instituting more uniform procedures for annual reviews of staff. Or the organization might be adding a senior management tier, putting distance between the ED and many of the staff who formerly reported to him or her. This can be threatening or alienating for staff who may have enjoyed the flexibility that comes with informality or the direct relationship with the ED. It is precisely at such moments that leaders' motives or priorities are questioned, rumors start circulating, and morale takes a dive. It is imperative that the ED assume responsibility during such points by doing the following:

1. Acknowledge the change and the trade-offs it presents. You are in fact changing the way you do business. Everyone will be better served by acknowledging this.

2. Place the change in the context of the broader vision, explaining how this particular change is a critical part of the larger change effort that will be in the organization's best interests.

3. Remind stakeholders of what will remain the same, regardless of the degree of change. This is where a well-articulated, widely embraced set of organizational values can be especially important. Clear values that resonate with staff and board can be an important anchor in turbulent times.

4. Be a champion of the change and stick to the message. Although groups are an essential element of organization development and change, it is also the case that people watch their leaders closely and follow their cues to understand what is valued (or not).

5. Build support and shared ownership among key stakeholders—both staff and board—for shepherding the change process. At the staff level, this may be an actual team, or it may simply be an understanding that the priorities of senior management have shifted to focus on the change efforts. At both the board and staff levels, it's important that there be as much shared responsibility and ownership as possible for the change effort, because leaders will inevitably face challenges from staff and board members who disagree with or are threatened by the change effort. Leaders' ability to

champion the effort and support each other when challenged is a critical component of success.

6. To achieve item 4, leaders need to empower staff appropriately. Part of the culture shift for the infrastructure organization can entail the ED's allowing the staff the authority and responsibility to manage departments, make important decisions, and otherwise take on greater leadership roles.

INFRASTRUCTURE INTERVIEW

Becky James-Hatter is the ED of Big Brothers Big Sisters of Eastern Missouri (BBBSEMO), one of four hundred affiliates of Big Brothers Big Sisters, the nation's oldest and largest mentoring organization. To say that Becky James-Hatter is passionate about the mission of BBBSEMO is like saying that Billie Holiday could sing or that Martha Stewart pays attention to detail. James-Hatter's commitment to accountability, the core values of the organization, and overall excellence are unflinching. Under James-Hatter's leadership, BBBSEMO has created an organizational culture that is very strong and has attained an impressive level of achievement. In 2010, BBBSEMO won four national awards for excellence awarded by Big Brothers Big Sisters: Agency of the Year; Board of the Year; Staff of the Year (Margaret Slack Award), co-awarded to two staff members; and #1 Quality Award (based on the previous year's program performance). BBBSEMO is the first Big Brothers Big Sisters affiliate to win all four awards in one year.

We chose to include the story of James-Hatter and BBBSEMO in this book because it offers an example of an organization that successfully navigated the infrastructure phase, particularly with regard to three of the key themes in this chapter: the role of the board-ED relationship, the importance of organizational culture, and the power of adaptive leadership.

Let's start by talking about what is at the core of BBBSEMO.

To build trusting and enduring relationships that encourage and support young people. At the individual level, we fulfill our mission through any great relationship or service or love that an individual child has gotten. That brings me all the joy. On a broader level, the complete joy of innovation, trying to crack the code, figure it out. The relationships that the staff and board have, among ourselves and in the community. How powerful and meaningful they are. Nothing comes even close.

What would you define as critical moments for the organization?

One big moment of transformation for me was when three of my staff quit at the same time. I realized that the problem was that the pressure to achieve our target numbers for matches was creating a lot of stress for staff, which was leading to staff turnover. And it was leading to turnover in our matches as well; the retention rates of our "Bigs" were not near what we wanted and needed them to be. We woke up and realized that the key to our success was in the quality of the relationships. This organization is built on relationships, but most important was the quality of relationship between each Big and Little. We made a commitment that our target numbers (of Big-Little relationships) would not exceed the number of high-quality relationships that we thought we could help to build and sustain. Today, we have the highest retention rates in the Big Brother Big Sister network.

So you had to go back to the core before you could think about growth?

Yes. And that made all the difference for us. There are things we just will not do. I have been working at this for sixteen years, and sometimes we lost our way and had to find it back. Now it's codified and we're less likely to. This is who we are, and that is enormously powerful. The whole organization knows it, and the community will know it.

How would you define the culture of BBBSEMO?

We say that our one core value is accountability. We are accountable first and foremost to the children and youth and our program members and their families. We are accountable to our board through the results of our work. And we are accountable to our donors as well.

But we are also, as a staff, accountable to each other. If I am not performing as I should be, my staff knows that I expect them to hold me accountable for that. And they know that I will listen to what they say, take it seriously, and do my best to address the issue. Likewise, if I see someone who's in distress and don't help them, I've made a bad decision for this organization. I'm accountable for people's spirit. Everything that happens here, we co-own. We need to tell each other the truth.

This is a very entrepreneurial culture. We don't have job descriptions; we have scorecards that are directly tied to annual plan goals, cultural competencies, and job competencies. Another aspect of our culture is curiosity. There is a curiosity in trying to become a better and more effective organization. We've been trying to figure out the "ABCs" on our Littles and how we are going to collect and reflect that information. We have new software that helps us understand what is going on with the kids. We have curiosity to look at the data and see what is going on.

The other word that is emerging for us is "intrapreneur": an inner entrepreneur. I need a staff of intrapreneurs—people who are willing to take risks. This is also true on our board. It's who we are.

We believe in the BoardSource premise that a strong, trusting relationship between the board and ED is pivotal to board excellence and, by extension, organizational success. Can you talk a little bit about how this has evolved at BBBSEMO?

Trust is everything to us here. We can have very candid discussions. It's not controlling. I've never had a board crisis in sixteen years. Our board is a combination of smarts and scrappy. Trust, curiosity, and accountability. I work with them at a very high level. I need them to be smarter and bigger than the staff.

The board looks at the strategic vision, understands where the organization is going, listens to what the staff needs, and tries to figure out how to help. They ask questions and will challenge us from time to time on our strategy. Now, with our new strategic plan in place, the staff and I are challenged in a whole new set of ways. I can go to the board with questions or recommendations, and they can give me value-added feedback. The one thing that we've always had with the board is that we are very results oriented. We have to get things done. And together we've consistently delivered. We fulfill the promise to each other. The results orientation has kept us very focused.

CCAT Findings: Infrastructure

A review of the 435 organizations in TCC Group's CCAT database in the infrastructure stage found that, on average, organizations were strong in the following areas (strength being defined as a score of 220 or above out of 300):

Adaptive

Environmental learning: using collaboration and networking with community leaders and funders to learn about what's going on in the community and stay current with what is going on in the field.

Leadership

Internal leadership: organizational leaders apply a mission-centered, focused, and inclusive approach to making decisions, as well as inspiring and motivating people to act upon them.

Leader vision: organizational leaders apply a mission-centered, focused, and inclusive approach to making decisions, as well as inspiring and motivating people to act upon them.

Management

Managing program staff: managing to ensure that program staff have the knowledge, skills, and cultural sensitivity to effectively deliver services.

Manager-to-staff communications: open channels of communication between managers and staff, including how open managers are to constructive feedback.

Organizational Culture

Empowering: promoting proactivity, learning, and a belief in the value and ability of staff and clients.

Challenges included the following (challenge being defined as a score of 190 or less out of 300):

Adaptive

Organizational learning: self-assessing, using assessment data/findings to conduct strategic planning, and following through on strategic plans.

Program resource adaptability: easily adapting to changes in program resources, including funding and staff.

Leadership

Leadership sustainability: cultivating organizational leaders, avoiding an overreliance on one leader, and planning for leadership transition (including having a succession plan).

Technical

Technology skills: ability to run efficient operations.

Program evaluation skills: ability to design and implement an effective evaluation.

Marketing skills: ability to communicate effectively with stakeholders, internal and external.

Fundraising skills: ability to develop the necessary resources for efficient operations, including the management of donor relations.

Source: TCC Group.

chapter FOUR

Maturity/Impact Expansion (MIE)

What happens to the nonprofit after it "graduates" from infrastructure and "grows out" of adolescence? In the Stevens framework (see Figure 1.1), the mature organization is one where both programs and operations are well established and working well.

Having survived adolescence, the mature organization is clear about who it is and what it does, and it has developed the infrastructure needed to do its work consistently well. The program model is well defined. There is a professional staff led by a visionary executive director (ED). Staff and board responsibilities are clearly delineated. The board leaves the running of the organization to staff and focuses its time and energy on its governance role, including such functions as approving and monitoring the budget, setting policy, evaluating the ED, supporting fundraising activities, and representing the organization to external audiences.

The Stevens model offers a compelling goal for nonprofits that seek to move up the lifecycle. It embodies the vision statement that we discussed in Chapters Two and Three, in that it provides a picture of a strong, stable organization. What the Stevens model doesn't address, however, is the concept of impact. It is not enough for an organization to strive for stable programs and systems; those programs and systems exist in service to something bigger: achieving mission, or impact. In recognition of this third element, the top tier of the TCC Group lifecycle is called "impact expansion" (see Figure 1.2).

This phase of the lifecycle assumes that certain thresholds in core program and infrastructure have been achieved. In addition to having achieved stability, the impact expansion organization is at a point where its programs have demonstrated effectiveness, and the lessons learned by the nonprofit are being leveraged for continuous improvement within the organization (such as by using evaluation data to improve programs or employing strategic planning processes to increase the efficiency of operations) and to benefit peer organizations or the broader field (such as by presenting findings at conferences, providing technical assistance, or participating in coalitions).

Although organization in the maturity/impact expansion (MIE) phase may appear to have everything all figured out, it has to work at least as hard as its colleagues in other phases of the lifecycle. The challenge for the MIE organization is to expand on its achievements, to continue to improve, and to maximize impact by sharing its knowledge and expertise with external stakeholders.

How does the high-arc/low-arc model apply to the MIE organization? The question for an organization at this phase is not *when* the organization will begin to decline, but *whether* it will do so. The high-arc/low-arc concept might be best understood as a caution to organizations that are at the top of the lifecycle or pyramid. Their challenge is to recognize what they have achieved and to continue to improve. The model would predict that the low-arc organization would have a greater likelihood of expanding its position at the top, because it was more deliberate in its growth. The low-arc organization (Figure 4.1) has likely

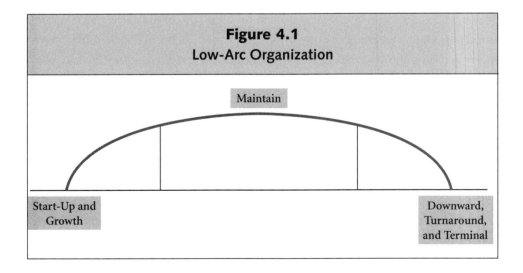

Figure 4.1
Low-Arc Organization

Maintain

Start-Up and Growth

Downward, Turnaround, and Terminal

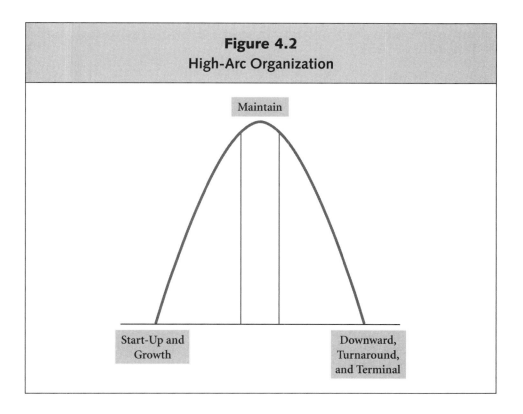

Figure 4.2
High-Arc Organization

Maintain

Start-Up and Growth

Downward, Turnaround, and Terminal

had a long-standing commitment to programmatic quality and impact. This organization is less likely to engage in growth for growth's sake and is more rigorous in applying criteria related to quality, outcomes, and mission achievement.

The model also assumes that the organization with a steeper growth trajectory (Figure 4.2) might find it more difficult to fully absorb its gains. Growth probably occurred too rapidly for the organization to be able to absorb and institutionalize it. This organization might find itself in decline after a relatively short period. Its ability to engage in a successful turnaround phase will depend, at least in part, on slowing down the rate of growth and change—on "lowering" its arc.

In the next section, we are going to focus our discussion on resource development. To be financially successful, nonprofits need to take the low-arc approach to resource acquisition, and they need to envision this function more broadly and more deeply than as simply fundraising. We use the term *resource development* to encompass the various types of support that an organization needs to cultivate.

IMPORTANCE OF RESOURCE DEVELOPMENT IN THE MIE PHASE

We have worked with dozens of nonprofit organizations in many capacities: as program participants, volunteers, staff, managers, executives, and board members. In all that time, we have never once heard the leader of a nonprofit client declare, "We have enough money." We might argue that the central challenge to organizations is reaching the MIE phase, which we see manifested in many ways:

- Resource-strapped nonprofits are not structured in ways that facilitate development of meaningful relationships with peer organizations. For those that manage to build collegial relationships that allow exchange of information, it is the rare nonprofit that collaborates meaningfully with peers by sharing human resources, space, or equipment, or that works together toward a common goal, even when it might be in their best interest to do so.

- Many of the nonprofits we've worked with consider themselves the "best-kept secret" in their community. They have dozens of examples of excellence, personal transformation, or community change; yet these stories, which have great potential to appeal to donors, too often go untold in ways that convey the power of the organization behind them. And reaching donors is just the beginning. Too few nonprofits develop the types of external relationships that broaden their circle of supporters, increase their visibility, and attract interest and attention to broader systemic interests of concern.

- Organizations often ask for additional resources before fully appreciating and leveraging what they already have at their disposal. Can staff be deployed more efficiently? Can they leverage their Web site to engage audiences in new ways?

York's Sustainability Formula grew out of a single question: What predicts organizational sustainability?[1] His study found that fully 30 percent of the organizations in the database perceived themselves to be "challenged" in this regard, and 28 percent regarded themselves as "strong." Looking at the variables that characterized the strong organizations, York found that among the most important predictors of sustainability are

1. Strong leadership (defined as strong internal leadership and leader vision)
2. Fundraising capacity
3. Financial management

York emphasizes that fundraising capacity and financial management are only predictors of MIE when accompanied by strong leadership. What is the connection between leadership and fundraising? York suggests that, in large part, it's the ability of senior staff and board members to communicate compelling messages to external stakeholders, cultivate relationships with donors, and be strategic in the creation of other partnerships that will ultimately bring new information and financial resources into the organization. In other words, effective leaders are those who demonstrate strong adaptive capacity (defined as the ability to monitor, assess, respond to, and stimulate internal and external changes).

When we seek to understand the source of our clients' frustrations with fundraising, we often hear about the challenges involved in implementing an often diffuse series of activities that may include writing proposals, planning events, or pursuing new sources of public funding. To be clear, we appreciate the importance of fundraising. We understand that nonprofits need decent databases, people who can write proposals, and the checks that come from an annual campaign. What we don't hear much about, typically, is the overall strategy that is guiding their effort.

Why does strategy matter? Consider the challenges facing nonprofits:

1. The environment is a very competitive one. Between 1998 and 2005, the number of U.S. nonprofits grew from 1.1 million to 1.5 million. Of these, approximately 1 million are public charities, meaning that they derive their funding from multiple sources.

2. The Great Recession, from which the U.S. economy appears to be emerging, has severely reduced the funds available to many nonprofits. Although the stock market has returned many endowments to precrash levels, unemployment remains high. And with many states in true budgetary crisis, the conventional wisdom is that the worst is yet to come for organizations that contract with government agencies.

3. As competition increases and financial resources remain at best uncertain, nonprofits are struggling to keep up with growing demands to demonstrate accountability to funders by providing data about the results of their investments. This invariably entails some level of investment on the part of the nonprofit in the collection, interpretation, and analysis of data.

This list represents just the tip of the iceberg when it comes to the challenges facing nonprofits seeking funds. We believe that a clear and well-conceived strategy is the best defense and the best offense. Obtaining resources is a not a quick, one-time activity; it is a marathon, not a sprint. Nonprofits need a solid long-term approach to compete more effectively, one that is well integrated with other core functions, particularly programs. What a long-term perspective and a solid, well-integrated strategy require is strong leadership that can connect the dots between vision, organizational strengths, and resource development. In the remainder of this chapter, we will focus on two aspects of how leadership is manifested in resource development: making the case and effective collaboration.

MAKING THE CASE

If we were trying to obtain funding for your mission, the first question to be asked is, "Why fund your work?" Or even better, "Why fund anything?" When teaching aspiring fund developers, John often asks them to envision the desk of a foundation program officer the day after a deadline. The desk is covered with aspiring proposals citing their great reasons for why the foundation should fund their organization. Most of these proposals will not include the most important information: what distinguishes them from their competition. In the nonprofit world, we talk about a case statement. In the private sector, the analogous concept is the value proposition. Whatever the term, it is incumbent on nonprofit leaders to articulate their unique value. Having data to document programmatic quality and impact is an increasingly important component of an organization's ability to make a compelling case for itself. It is also important to communicate how your plans for your project are different from other efforts that exist. How is your tutoring program distinguished from its competition?

A first step is to identify your strengths. John recently participated in a meeting where the facilitator used an icebreaker exercise that required the group to write five things that "are great about us." Most in the room had a very difficult time answering this question. The reason is that individuals can have a challenging time listing the positive before the negative. Organizations also have the same difficulty. It is far easier to list what the needs and challenges of the organizations are before the assets. In order to make a stronger case, organizations must start by listing their assets.

The next step is to document these strengths. A nonprofit's biggest asset is the value of its mission, measured in terms of program quality and impact. Some examples of measures that help a nonprofit tell this story include

- Qualitative data, or case studies, that highlight individual success stories and how they typify the work of the organization.

- Quantitative data, such as concrete measures of success, that the organization can tie to its own work, such as job retention data, increased school attendance, or increased subscription rates for a local performing arts organization.

- Information that highlights the ways in which your organization provides its programs and services in a high-quality manner. Are your programs fully subscribed? How do others perceive your organization? Are your programs based on research or aligned with the most current thinking about "best practice"?

In Chapter Two, we talked about the value of a logic model in helping nonprofits articulate, understand, and refine their program strategy. Logic models actually originated from a program evaluation methodology. By using outcomes to connect mission impact with program strategy, the logic model is a very powerful way for nonprofits to develop their evaluation frameworks. The outcomes become measurements of the change that was effected; quality is measured by looking for connections between strategy and outcomes. Having data that document "what works, and why" is a powerful way to make the case to a funder. But even for those groups that cannot evaluate their programs, we believe that the logic model remains a powerful and valuable tool. Going through the steps of systematically thinking through what you hope to achieve and how you are going to do it inspires a lot of good discussion and forces stakeholders to state their underlying assumptions. This level of care and thought can, on its own, put you head and shoulders above your competition.

Maximizing Efficiency

Another common question John asks when training groups is, "If I gave you a million dollars, what would you use the money for?" Surprisingly, most people in the room are hard-pressed to answer the question. Often an organization begins the process of asking for funds without a clear picture of where to apply those funds. Further, organizations very often already have the resources right under their organizational umbrella to meet their needs.

One of the first actions that should be undertaken when pinpointing the exact areas that need to be funded is conducting an asset inventory. Simply put, you should list all the resources that live under the organization's umbrella and map those resources to the programs they support. Attaching those listed resources to the goals and directions of the organization will do two things. It should show what assets are being used by what program, and, more important, it should show what assets the organization *does not* have to fulfill its mission completely.

For example, suppose that your organization believes it needs three additional staff members for a new program. Through the asset inventory exercise, you find that you have several staff members who are looking for additional opportunities and responsibilities and believe they can partly fill these positions or roles. Previously, departments may not have cross-shared these existing assets, and now these assets can be used to offset needs and propel the organization. In addition, the budget outlines the areas where the organization needs to raise the remaining necessary resources to sustain its mission.

Looking at the following budget template (Table 4.1), the exercise becomes one of listing all the sections of a potential or existing budget. The first column is the organization contribution or internal assets we've discussed here. Listing all of the organizational assets down the first column will allow the organization to see, through a budget, what assets it has.

Generating Interest and Enhancing Your Reputation

Another strategy an organization can use to push itself to the top of the funder list is to create a "bandwagon" of meaningful partnerships and community connections which showcase that others believe in your efforts. An additional benefit of creating these relationships is that funders will also want a relationship with the effort because they see others engaged and want to join the bandwagon.

We have also found that organizations that are able to remain in the MIE phase tend to have leaders who understand that their role is largely concerned with what happens outside the organization's offices or program sites. Consider this observation from the ED of a large, growing, and programmatically successful nonprofit: "I have come to see that, as we grow, our organization isn't a business, it's a campaign, and you are always driving it. If you don't know how to politic and campaign and organize you can't move. The ones that fail are the ones that look inward."

	Organizational Contribution	Other Funding Sources	Funder Request	TOTAL
Personnel Expenses				
Staff Costs				
Position Title				
Position Title				
Staff Costs Subtotal				
Fringe Benefits				
Fringe Benefits Subtotal				
TOTAL PERSONNEL EXPENSES				
Nonpersonnel Expenses				
Office Space				
Rent				
Utilities				
Furnishings				
Maintenance				
Insurance				
Office Space Subtotal				
Equipment/Supplies				
Office Supplies				
Printing				
Postage and Delivery				
Copier				
Phone/Fax				
Repairs/Maintenance				
Computer Supplies				
Equipment/Supplies Subtotal				
Travel-Related Expenses				
Air Travel				
Travel—Lodging				
Travel—Mileage				
Meetings/Seminars/Conferences				
Travel-Related Subtotal				
TOTAL NONPERSONNEL EXPENSES				
TOTAL DIRECT COSTS				
Overhead Expenses/Indirect Costs				
PROJECT TOTAL:				

TABLE 4.1
Budget Template

Are your staff and volunteer leaders well-known and highly regarded? Does your ED have a strong network of peers and good relationships with the press? Organizations cannot exist in a vacuum; our experience has been that, assuming the nonprofit has achieved a critical level of programmatic and organizational excellence, it will thrive when its ED can spend increasing amounts of time developing external relationships.

BUILDING BOARD ACCOUNTABILITY IN THE MIE PHASE

The challenge for organizations in the MIE phase is to avoid complacency. This applies to all facets of the organization, including the board. Boards that were energized during periods of growth can become detached during the MIE phase, sometimes becoming a group that lives off the success of the past by engaging in rubber-stamping actions in the present.

Every leadership and self-help book in the world addresses to some extent the importance of setting goals and having a structure in place to hold you to your goals, but what process exists to help board members do the same? Considering that being a board member is advanced voluntarism with major responsibility, shouldn't there be a process or tool that helps board members stay on task and develop in their role?

Grading Board Efforts

One very effective tool to help hold board members accountable is the Board Report Card, developed by Harlem RBI, a nonprofit organization in New York City, whose mission is to provide inner-city youth with opportunities to play, learn, and grow, using the power of teams to coach, teach, and inspire youth to recognize their potential and realize their dreams. A sample report card is illustrated in Table 4.2.

Although this tool is called a report card, the board member does not get a grade, but will be able to instantly determine whether she is performing or not. The report card allows board members to set goals relating to the areas that are most important to the whole board, compare their development to their previous year's performance, and outline their goals for the current year. Board member goals reflect the organization's strategic goals and can be adjusted as priorities shift. For example, the board may find that board members are attending external community events to talk about the organization and "sell" its programs. If that is the case, they would add a category like "Community Events Attended." The following are the items and categories outlined in the Harlem RBI Board Report Card, with some additional discussion:

TABLE 4.2
Sample Board Report Card

Board of Director Member: _____
Summary of Activities for: XXX, **member since January 2006**
Term Ends: 2012
2006 Committee Recommendation: **Development, Executive**

	2010	2011
Avg. Board Attendance:	xx%	xx%
Avg. Board Gift:	$xx,xxx	$xx,xxx
Meeting Attendance:	4 of 4 (100%)	3 of 4 (75%)—1 by phone
Giving:	$4,450 (Campaign 2)	$9,000 (Campaigns 2 & 4)
Getting:	+$100,000 (Campaigns 1 & 2) (Company A, B, C, D, E, F)	+$200,000 (Campaigns 1 & 2) (Company A, B, C, D, E, F, G, H, I)
Committee Participation:	Member, Development Committee	Member, Development Committee
Committee Attendance:	Development: no meetings	N/A
Event Participation:	(3 of 5) Event 1, 3, 5	Event 1 Honoree
Program Visits:	1 (Open House)	2 (Open House and Neighborhood Cleanup)
Other:		
Stated Goals for 2010:	Continues to leverage his professional and personal relationships for agency, most notably securing lead Gala honoree. Company remains major supporter of Campaign/Event.	
Stated Goals for 2011:	Goal for 2011 is to keep it up. Fine with remaining on the Development Committee, as we suggest. (Expressed his strong preference that everyone attends meetings in person and not by phone.)	

Term Ends   If the board has term limits, it might be important to note this. For example, if a board member is in the final year of his service and has the opportunity to be voted in for a second term, then his performance may have an impact on whether or not he is voted to stay on the board.

Average Board Attendance   Board members do have to attend board meetings, so having a line item giving them an understanding of how the overall board is performing in terms of board attendance can help individual board members understand how they are performing compared to the board as a whole. Further, if this attendance figure is low, the information could supplement a conversation on how an individual board member might be helpful in getting lower-performing board members to the meetings.

Average Board Gift   This figure provides a general view of members' giving. There may be some sensitivity with regard to this topic, in that many board members might not be brought on because of the size of their gift but on the basis of their offering expertise or a particular perspective. This item could be restated to align more closely with your nonprofit's expectations related to giving, but remember that typically a board member's central role in an organization is to monitor and raise money. A final observation: sometimes nothing motivates board members more than competition. A member's discovering that he is performing below the average can be a great motivator for him to bring in more dollars.

Meeting Attendance   This figure is expressed as a percentage: how many meetings were attended out of the total number held. As you can see in Table 4.2, Harlem RBI makes note of whether the member attended the meeting in person or by phone. If you find that a member is attending a majority of meetings by phone, you may want to address the subject with the board member specifically.

Giving and Getting   These categories list the individual member's giving and the amount she brought to the organization. Again, this is a sensitive area; it may be more important to look at the *number* of gifts obtained. Also, some members may be better in one category than in the other, so you may want to include a total of the two. Harlem RBI breaks them into individual categories and also cites which campaign(s) the board member gave to. Depending on how much information your board members will need, you can decide to include more details or stay with one simple number.

Committee Participation and Attendance   As board members are assigned or sign up for committees, oftentimes committees can become the work of just a few individuals who serve on a number of committees. If your board's committee work is considered important, then individual members' attendance should be tracked and recorded.

Event Participation   Because board members are community champions for the organization, members' attendance at critical events—being front and center when the community is present—is important. The Harlem RBI's Report Card records which specific events the board member attended.

Program Visits   Many organizations find it important for board members to understand the programs by seeing them firsthand. Some want board members to establish a deeper relationship with the programs, including by volunteering in a program on a regular basis. As you can see in Table 4.2, there were specific formal events during which this board member interacted with programs. Organizations may make it mandatory that each year board members attend a specific programming event, one that might be a central part of the organizational culture.

Other   This is where you list anything the board member did for the organization that was outside the categories for which he is being evaluated. For example, a board member may have connected the organization to a new community partner or had a colleague provide some pro bono Web site development work for the organization.

Stated Goals   This is an opportunity for the board member to cite what she hopes to achieve in the coming year and also to reflect on the goals she set for the previous year, seeing if she reached her goals and, it is hoped, using that historical data to inform the content of her future goals.

How the Board Report Card Should Be Used

The purpose of the report card is to help board members set realistic but ambitious goals for themselves and to have a mechanism in place to hold them accountable for reaching their goals. The following are additional points to keep in mind as your organization begins to use the report card.

Private Not Public   Board members can be competitive, and sometimes that competition can be a positive motivator to raising dollars, but the report card should not be treated as a public document for all to see. It is intended for the eyes of the board chair, the ED, and, if one exists, the governance committee chair. It should be used to help guide the board member and also as an aid in a difficult conversation with a board member who is underperforming. In fact, because board members use the card to chart their own path to success, it offers a degree of objectivity to the discussion in cases of underperformance.

Discussion Facilitator   Often a review of the completed report card indicates that the board member could be perceived as having more capacity in certain areas. For example, if a board member was recently awarded a new, high-paying job, then one might expect that he could be making a larger gift in the future. Of course, this is an assumption, so using the report card to discuss goals is a good way to ascertain the limits of an individual board member. She may reveal that the new job is great, but that she also has committed to starting a bed-and-breakfast that is getting off the ground.

Not a Pink Slip   If a board member is underperforming and the report card shows it, the natural impulse is to use the card as a way to show the member the door. *This would be a mistake.* The report card is a tool to help set goals and establish MIE-phase accountability; if a board member is underperforming, he already knows it and does not need someone to flash the report card in front of his face. Even though he may not be pulling his weight, he is or potentially will be a future asset to the organization. Use the report card as a way to find another avenue in which this member can help. Maybe being a board member is not for him at this point; he can still be a volunteer or serve on a less burdensome committee or just help in smaller ways, such as by using his network to assist the organization in meeting new and interesting partners. Using the report card to do anything other than facilitating the relationship could prove harmful to the organization in the future.

Rich Berlin, the ED of Harlem RBI, noted that the report card is valuable not just in holding board members accountable, but also in aiding in the process of recruiting and screening potential board members. Once prospective members see the report card, they can decide whether they can fulfill the duties expected of them. The report card also helps ensure that those who are voted onto the board are committed, engaged, and ready to step up. Berlin notes that as Harlem RBI's board becomes stronger as an entity, his list of "rock stars" who would like to join continues to grow.

ORGANIZATIONAL ASSESSMENT: THE CSE TOOL

The Core Support Evaluation (CSE) is designed to assist organizations in understanding their current challenges, developing a plan to alleviate those challenges, and expending the appropriate amount of time and energy on those solutions. Adapted from feedback structures designed in the defense industry, the CSE will benefit a variety of areas within a nonprofit organization, including board development, human capital management, nonprofit risk aversion, and resource allocation. The following sections discuss the CSE and how an organization can use it; Table 4.3 is an example.

As you can see from Table 4.3, the CSE tool operates as a dashboard; it can be applied to an individual employee, a program or division, or the entire organization. In the latter case, the ED can use the CSE almost as a State of the Union report to the board on where the organization currently stands. In the table, there are several important areas that are interrelated to make the dashboard work. Those areas are as follows:

The Legend

In the top left-hand corner of the dashboard page is a legend that outlines the color-coding system. These colors correspond to positions or feelings that the evaluator has with regard to how that particular area of the organization is performing. Choosing the colors for these areas can serve as a powerful ongoing exercise in having individuals, departments, and the organization become clear on obtaining consensus on how they are performing. The following paragraphs outline the legend categories:

Blue   Blue means that the individual, program, or organization is performing at the highest level, achieving optimal impact, or both. Although you may have an impulse to highlight many areas blue to show that there are a number of high-performing areas, in reality there should be few blue areas cited. Blue should be reserved for when the effort has achieved a high-level award or has achieved a very tough goal that is rarely met. Receiving a Rose Garden event in your honor at the White House should obtain a blue—not, for example, full program attendance. If blue is overused, the other ratings become less related to the actual situation they represent. If blue were to represent that all program staff came to the staff meetings on time, then what would be normal, or the status quo? It is important to make sure that the blue designation represents a real honor.

TABLE 4.3

Sample Core Support Evaluation (CSE)

	Performance	Human Capital	Systems and Processes	Tools	Client Satisfaction	Notes
Finance	RED	YELLOW	RED	YELLOW	YELLOW	Delay in submissions; instances of leaving dollars on table.
Operations	YELLOW	YELLOW	GREEN	RED	GREEN	Significant space and technology challenges.
Evaluation	GREEN	YELLOW	GREEN	RED	GREEN	Delayed database purchase; not able to adequately track key mission items.
Human Resources	GREEN	YELLOW	YELLOW	GREEN	GREEN	Onboarding process needs to improve.
Development	BLUE	GREEN	GREEN	YELLOW	BLUE	Exceeded fundraising goal in gala; increased revenue.
Program A	GREEN	YELLOW	YELLOW	GREEN	YELLOW	Program leadership turnover; professionalism of part-time staff at Site AB.
Program B	YELLOW	YELLOW	GREEN	YELLOW	GREEN	Not able to hire several positions this year; part-time hire challenges.
Program C	BLUE	GREEN	GREEN	YELLOW	BLUE	Returned 5 million to community with reduced budget in FY09.
Strategic Planning Area A	GREEN	GREEN	GREEN	GREEN	GREEN	Strategic Planning Area is "stronger community outreach." Starting initiative.
Organizational Value Area A	GREEN	GREEN	YELLOW	GREEN	YELLOW	Organizational Value Area is "clients feel part of organizational direction." Client feedback forms have not been used.

Legend

BLUE — Performance causing frequent and/or significant achievements beyond expectations

YELLOW — Performance causing minor, isolated impediments to achieving program objectives or trends indicating potential for doing so in future

RED — Performance causing repeated or severe impediments to achieving program objectives

GREEN — Good performance

WHITE — Skill not exercised in current workload

Green Green means that the performance was good, or the status quo. As the organization should always be performing well, green is the color that represents that the effort is operating on par with the high expectations the effort has set for itself. If there were no challenges to discuss and all areas were being met, then the dashboard would show all green; however, this is a rarity, as no organization, program, or individual is without at least some minor challenges to report.

Yellow Yellow is the caution designation, appropriate if the individual is unable to meet his or her job performance expectations, or the program is having a tough time obtaining enough program participants to register for the program, or the organization is experiencing challenges related to recruiting the right people for its services. A yellow rating alerts you to where the challenges are before they become more serious and also highlights common threads. For example, let's say a dashboard has several yellow boxes, and, looking at each yellow box, you notice that there is a technology problem associated with it. In this case, it may be that the issue can be solved not with seven individual solutions, but in a smaller number of solutions aimed at the common technology challenges.

Red A red designation means what red always means: concern or danger. As the legend notes, red indicates performance causing repeated or severe impediments to achieving program objectives. Like blue, red should be used rarely: only when the area is in serious disarray, meaning that the organization could close or be sued, or the individual could be fired. For example, if the organization has only enough money for two payrolls or a child fell off the monkey bars and severely hurt herself, these areas are red.

White A white designation means that there are no data at hand to give the area any feedback or that the specific area is not currently being exercised. White, like blue and red, should be used infrequently. If used often, then the area listed in the left-hand column should be discarded for one that is more aligned to the organization, program, or individual.

The Issue Areas

Identifying the issue areas—the items listed in the left-hand column—is a very specific function; and across the organization, if there are multiple dashboards in play, not one should look alike. The work of the ED is different from that of the vice president of programs, which is different from that of the program coordinator, and so on. Identifying these categories becomes a dialogue on the most important areas that make up the work that an individual, department, and ultimately an organization does. Our example illustrates a typical organizational dashboard, which might list seven to fifteen key areas that the ED and board have decided are important when looking at the organization as a whole; this example shows ten specific issue areas. As we've noted, these areas could instead include information for a specific program or site location, outlining the dozen or so components that are most important when thinking about that effort; the dashboard can also be used to outline the work of an individual employee, in which case you could use the items listed in an employee's job description as the issue areas.

As you will notice in our example, the bottom two cells in the left-hand column identify a strategic planning area and an organizational value area. One of the challenges to strategic plans or in having organizational values is that they often don't live on after the process is completed or the values are printed on the fancy paper. To ensure that these areas are addressed within the organization, make sure they are intertwined with the organization's major current: the employees. Approximately 80 percent of organizational funding is spent on staffing, so if you want to ensure that your nonprofit's vision and values are breathing throughout the organization daily, tie them closely to human performance.

The Impact Areas

To understand how an organization is performing, one must first identify what areas are relevant to measure. These areas are then listed as the dashboard column headings, and the areas in the left-hand column are evaluated against them. The impact areas are as follows:

Performance   How is the project or program performing? Are the costs too high? Does the project or program schedule work? Are there specific issues that are hindering the project or program performance? This area addresses costs or technical issues (excluding technology issues) that hinder performance.

Human Capital   This column discusses the ability or inability of staff to meet the needs of those areas listed in the left-hand column. Does the area listed in each row have the right people aboard to perform? Perhaps you have enough staff, but the staff need training to perform in the areas listed. Is there training available to help staff meet these needs?

Systems and Processes Processes are the operating procedures or rules that are in place to help the items in the left-hand column come to fruition. For example, is there a form missing that would help navigate a process more clearly? If this area is organizational finance, for example, is there an issue with how the financial information is received or sent? This column relates to the transfer of information and the systems that are (or are not) in place to help move efforts forward.

Tools A major source of frustration for staff members in any organization, public or private, is in the technology and tools that are required to perform the necessary tasks. Are you trying to write a report, but the computer does not have the software needed? Or are you running an environmental science program, but do not have the necessary tools to conduct the experiments? This column is geared to discussing whether or not the organization has the proper technology or tools required to follow through on organizational, program, or individual duties.

Client Satisfaction Customer service relates to those for whom the organization, program, or individual is directing the mission of the organization—a program participant, community member, or client. A customer could also be a partner of the organization or a group that is providing a resource, such as a foundation, government contractor, or individual donor. If one or more of these groups provides feedback relating to challenges or excitement about one of the areas listed in the left-hand column, then this area can be color coded based on that feedback. Often these boxes are left white, which means that there are no proper feedback loops to inform the organization, program, or individual as to whether the customer is pleased or dissatisfied with the offering. If this is the case, the organization should code the white boxes yellow and begin work toward obtaining the proper feedback necessary to inform them of the customer's feelings with regard to the area.

The Action Steps Sheet

The second sheet of the CSE (Table 4.4), is the opportunity for the individual, department, and organization to outline how they are going to turn the yellow and red categories green. A dashboard is only as good as the action plan that moves the challenging areas to success. The following are the areas that make up the CSE action steps:

TABLE 4.4

Sample CSE Action Steps

Area	Color (Yellow, Red)	Reason for Yellow or Red	Recovery Steps	Anticipated Date Green
Finance	Yellow, red	Cash flow	• Financial consulting firm has been secured for up to 6 months.	• 6 months
Operations	Yellow, red	• Ongoing space challenges; overall concerns about office environment • Lack of formalized technology systems	• Potential facilities are being explored. • Assessment of operations is taking place to maximize productivity.	• 3 months • 6 months
Evaluation	Red	• Delay of database purchase	• Mapping project of neighborhood begins. • Database purchase has been placed on funding priority list.	• 6 months • 12 months
Human Resources	Yellow	• Department only has one employee due to funding cuts • Able to proceed with core HR functions but not yet progressed to higher-level talent management functions	• Assessment of department is taking place with support of consultant.	• 3 to 5 months

Area   This column refers to any of the areas on the dashboard that received either a yellow or red rating. In the example, finance, operations, evaluation, and human resources are listed as cited areas.

Color   This column indicates the color that the category has received. The only options are yellow or red.

Reason for Yellow or Red   In this column, you outline the exact reasons why the current area is yellow or red. In the example, for the finance area, the issue of cash flow is cited as the reason. Within this area, you may list a broad reason like cash flow or be more specific, saying, for example, "Revenue from government taking longer than expected due to state budget cuts." The audience may require more specifics; however, the CSE is not about crafting massive narratives but about giving concise, useful information in small spaces. The CSE should incite discussion, not end it; you will have time later to talk about solutions and to further discuss the reasoning behind why the area is yellow or red.

Recovery Steps   This column represents the "actions" behind the CSE action steps sheet; it allows the individual, department, and organization the opportunity to outline how they are going to solve the problem specifically. In our example, for the finance area, the recovery step was to bring in a financial consulting firm to help tackle the problem. If the issue were specifically due to late contract payments by the government, a specific action could be to press the state harder to make more timely payments or to involve the local elected official in helping secure payments. Although the main purpose of this column is to cite the specific solutions that are being offered to solve the problems, it should also stimulate important dialogue from others. Similar to the Reason for Yellow or Red column, Recovery Steps is meant to highlight the strategy for solving the issue so as to generate ideas and additional perspectives.

Anticipated Date Green   The last column cites an estimate of when the yellow or red will be green. This can be an important area because leaders often over- or underestimate these dates; again, filling in the column can be useful in encouraging discussion. If cash flow is red and you need the government payments to come on a more scheduled basis, then the green date will be either when the payments can be more formal or when the organization has enough funding in other areas that late payments will no longer be an issue.

One theme you may have noticed is that a primary function of the action sheet is to facilitate dialogue and bring to light people's expectations of one another. Where the executive views a yellow, the board may view a red; staff may view the action plan one way, the executive another. Employing the CSE will concentrate all parties on the specific issues that need to be addressed, put out unforeseen fires, and create collaborative solutions to meet the challenges of the organization.

IMPACT EXPANSION AND THE QUESTION OF SCALE

The term "going to scale" has become an increasingly important part of the discourse on the social sector in recent years. In our own consulting practices, we are frequently asked about how to help organizations take their effort to "the next level." Much of the discussion in the relatively new area of social entrepreneurship is about how to reach more people with an idea. One way to do this is through physical replication of programs. One might argue, for example, that the Girl Scouts or the YMCA are early examples of going to scale using a type of franchise model. A more expansive way to think about the question of scale is through the broader lens of replicating impact. The Spring 2010 issue of *Evaluation Exchange,* a periodical of the Harvard Family Research Project, points out that scaling is not just about serving more people but also about deepening or sustaining impact.[2] In the first of nine papers on "scaling what works," Grantmakers for Effective Organizations points out that "growing impact doesn't necessarily require organizational growth or the wholesale replication of programs—it may instead require expanding an idea or innovation, technology or skill, advocacy or policy change."[3]

The MIE organization is the place where the lifecycle and the question of scaling meet. Impact expansion is the phase in which scaling becomes relevant because the organization has established itself, both programmatically and organizationally. By the time an organization reaches the MIE phase, it has been able to test its strategies and has documented the quality and impact of its work.

Experts in the field agree that a strong theory of change (what we have referred to in this book as a logic model) is critical to determining whether an intervention should be replicated, how, and under what conditions. The theory of change (TOC) is the foundation for testing what works, and why. It is critical for evaluations to measure not only what worked (the outcomes) but also what contributed to the success (or failure) of an intervention. These factors are referred to as indicators of quality, and might include any of a vast number of variables. According to ActKnowledge, an independent research and capacity building organization affiliated with the Center for Human Environments at the Graduate Center of the City University of New York, a TOC is a "specific and measurable description of a social change initiative that forms the basis for strategic planning, on-going decision-making and evaluation. The methodology used to create a Theory of Change is also usually referred to as a Theory of Change, or the Theory of Change approach or method. So, when you hear or say 'Theory of Change,' you may mean either the process or the result."[4] ActKnowledge offers a wonderful example of a TOC for the organization Project Superwomen (www.theoryofchange.org/pdf/Superwomen_Example. pdf); its TOC Web site (www.theoryofchange.org) also offers a more in-depth view of the TOC development process.

Like any good planning and evaluation method for social change, the TOC requires participants to be clear on long-term goals, identify measurable indicators of success, and formulate actions to achieve goals.

MIE INTERVIEW

Our interview in this chapter is with Carole Wacey, the ED of MOUSE, a nonprofit technology organization centered on education. Its organizational path is one of a growing nonprofit confronted with many of the opportunities and challenges that are intertwined with growing to scale, achieving impact, and managing growth.

MOUSE is an innovative youth development organization that empowers underserved students to provide technology support and leadership in their schools, supporting their academic and career success. MOUSE was founded in 1997 by Andrew Rasiej and Sarah Holloway, who, along with leaders from the high-tech community in New York City, spearheaded the process of wiring public schools for Internet access in Manhattan. MOUSE's first project brought more than two hundred volunteers together to wire Andrew Rasiej's neighborhood high school, Washington Irving High School. In order to coordinate volunteer efforts,

Andrew created a registration database matching his volunteers' varied skills with schools needing particular assistance. This database marked the birth of MOUSE, an organization that today serves tens of thousands of underserved youth in schools across the United States. The MOUSE Squad trains and supports students in managing leading-edge technical support help desks in their schools, improving the ability to use technology to enhance learning while also providing a powerful, hands-on twenty-first-century learning experience for students. The MOUSE Squad extends learning beyond the help desk by providing events, hands-on workshops, projects, and a collaborative online network of youth technology leaders.

Talk about the founding of MOUSE—why was it created, and what were its ambitions when it was started?

MOUSE was founded in 1997 by Andrew Rasiej, entrepreneur, and Sarah Holloway, the organization's founding executive director. At this time, Silicon Valley was booming. Andrew and Sarah saw a clear divide between, on the one hand, what was going on in Silicon Valley and the growing importance of technology and the Internet in the workplace and world and, on the other hand, what was happening—or not happening—in New York City's public schools. Along with leaders from the high-tech community in New York City, MOUSE launched by galvanizing volunteers to help wire the schools for Internet access. More than two hundred volunteers showed up at the first MOUSE wiring day at Washington Irving High School.

In order to coordinate volunteer efforts, Andrew created a registration database matching his volunteers' varied skills with schools needing particular assistance. This database marked the birth of MOUSE. The organization has evolved over the years in sync with the schools' and students' evolving needs—from wiring to teacher training in the early years to the organization's current focus on in-school tech support, twenty-first-century skill building, and college and career preparedness.

Talk about the ebbs and flows that have led the organization to its current position of growth—how did it get to this point? What were the phases that you went through to get here?

As I consider MOUSE's evolution over the past thirteen years, I see five distinct phases:

Phase I: Launch (1997). MOUSE was founded to address an urgent need to connect schools and students to the Information Age—specifically, wiring New York City's schools to the Internet. MOUSE was ahead of the curve in terms of tech nonprofits and was able to readily attract partners—especially from the local and growing and young technology sector.

Phase II: Tech Boom (1998–2001). In parallel with Silicon Valley, MOUSE continued to grow and support a variety of programs—Digital Media Contest, Girls and Technology, MOUSE Squad, Tech Source. This was a boom time for the organization, and tech companies and entrepreneurs continued to provide support and ideas. MOUSE began a formal relationship with the New York City Department of Education and the New York City Council as a valued partner.

Phase III: Tech Bubble Burst (2001–2003). In the post–9/11 environment in NYC (which included the bursting of the tech bubble), MOUSE looked to streamline its growing roster of programs and exit "start-up" mode. By focusing on what was truly the greatest need in the schools *and* on what the organization could uniquely deliver, the organization prioritized MOUSE Squad as the program to formalize and scale. MOUSE Squad, a student-run technical support help desk embedded in dozens of local schools, focused on student outcomes, schoolwide technical support, and technology cost savings.

Phase IV: Focus and (Opportunistic) Growth (2003–2010). As I joined MOUSE in 2003, this provided an opportunity to build on the foundation established by Sarah and Andrew. MOUSE began to build new partnerships and expand beyond New York into Chicago (in partnership with the Chicago Public Schools), California (in partnership with Aspiranet), and internationally (in partnership with Microsoft in over fifty-eight countries).

As part of a 2008 business planning process, MOUSE determined that New York City would be the lab where we would test and develop new programmatic elements; we would affiliate with partners who would manage MOUSE Squad in their communities; we would offer a MOUSE-in-a-Box program so that any school could pay a fee to participate in the programs and become part of the MOUSE network. We also planned to develop a free online version so any school could participate in the benefits of running a student-led help desk. This free online version would also be a terrific tool for MOUSE and our network partners to build new relationships and provide additional services to the schools who experiment with the free online version.

MOUSE worked to grow existing partnerships—Chase, New York City Council, UBS Financial. At the same time, MOUSE reached out to new partners—Best Buy Children's Foundation, CME Group Foundation, Polk Bros. Foundation, U.S. Department of Commerce (ARRA funds).

Phase V: Strategic Growth (2011 and beyond). As MOUSE explores responding to tremendous demand for our programs, the next phase will focus on developing a deliberate growth strategy that will support MOUSE's long-term growth. MOUSE is currently exploring a variety of avenues that will enable the program to be brought to scale. These avenues include social venture capital, fundraising (foundations, tech industry, government), partnership affiliation, sales. MOUSE will be exploring the opportunities and challenges for each avenue and will select the ones that most effectively help us to achieve our goal of supporting underserved youth.

What is the thought behind growing the organization? Why now, and what process did you go through that helped get you to this point?

Determining MOUSE's ongoing business planning strategy has never been more important in terms of management priority. With a challenging economic climate, this is an area of significant focus. Our business plan takes into consideration program expansion, student impact, packaging and licensing, and the value proposition (for investors and schools). In FY '08, MOUSE engaged in a comprehensive business planning process that was led by the MOUSE board of directors—specifically, the ad hoc business planning committee. Our business plan was vetted with over thirty external senior-level advisers to MOUSE during summer 2008. In the fall of 2008, as we prepared to launch our expansion campaign to raise $13 million, the country entered a recession, and we knew immediately that MOUSE needed to shift its course of action. Despite the changes in the economic climate, the underlying work that was prescribed as part of the business planning process continues to guide MOUSE's programmatic and partnership development. MOUSE learned how to effectively make the case for growth of our organization as an opportunity for investors. Our strategy for growth and scalability, which includes adding a free online version of our program and a MOUSE-in-a-Box version, is currently under development.

Since 2008, MOUSE programs have grown from 158 sites to 350 sites (120 percent) while our budget has remained relatively flat. This further demonstrates that growth of MOUSE programs offers efficiencies that will continue to grow. We know that there is tremendous demand for our programs and want to explore the different avenues for growth to support scale while retaining quality programs.

What are the risks in growing this organization and going to scale? What keeps you up at night as you think about this ambitious path?

The primary risks that MOUSE has identified include the following:

- Entrepreneurial growth compromises the core MOUSE mission of reaching underserved students

- Quality of programs compromised
- Funding shortfalls
- Insufficient board or staff capacity
- Difficult political and economic climate
- Demand outstrips capacity

As you think about scaling, what would success be in the short and long term?

Short-term success: MOUSE board, staff, and partners can outline a business plan that establishes optimistic but realistic goals for growth over the next five years.

Long-term success: MOUSE is able to develop relationships with new network partners to deliver MOUSE programs in a growing number of communities across the United States. For long-term scaling success, MOUSE will need to develop a multitiered approach including social venture capital, major foundation funding, corporate investment, government, and earned income. In addition, MOUSE would develop a relationship with a well-respected evaluation partner who can help MOUSE ensure that our programs are having the student impact that we are seeking.

CCAT Findings: MIE

A review of the 465 organizations in TCC Group's CCAT database in the impact expansion phase found that, on average, organizations were strong in the following areas (strength being defined as a score of 220 or above out of 300):

Adaptive

Decision-making tools: using important tools, resources, and inputs to make decisions (for example, in-house data, staff input, client input, and a written strategic plan)

Environmental learning: using collaboration and networking with community leaders and funders to learn about what's going on in the community and stay current with what is going on in the field

Leadership

Internal leadership: apply a mission-centered, focused, and inclusive approach to making decisions, as well as inspire and motivate people to act upon them

Leader vision: formulate a clear vision and motivate others to pursue it

Leader influence: ability to persuade board, staff, and community leaders or decision makers to take actions

Management

Assessing staff performance: detailing clear roles and responsibilities and assessing staff performance against those roles and responsibilities

Managing performance expectations: facilitating clear and realistic expectations among staff

Managing program staff: managing to ensure that program staff have the knowledge, skills, and cultural sensitivity to effectively deliver services

Volunteer management: recruiting, retaining, providing role clarity and direction, developing, valuing, and rewarding volunteers

Manager-to-staff communications: open channels of communication between managers and staff, including how open managers are to constructive feedback

Conveying unique value of staff: providing positive feedback, rewards, and time for reflection

Problem solving: effectively, judiciously, and consistently resolve human resource problems and interpersonal conflicts, including engaging staff in the problem-solving process

(continued)

Staff development: coaching, mentoring, training, and empowering staff to improve their skills and innovate

Financial management: managing organizational finances, including staff compensation

Technology

Service delivery skills: ability to ensure efficient and high-quality services

Program evaluation skills: ability to design and implement an effective evaluation

Organizational Culture

Unifying: engendering open and honest communication across all levels in the organization, leading to sense of cohesive "group identity"

Empowering: promoting proactivity, learning, and a belief in the value and ability of staff and clients

Challenges included the following (challenge being defined as a score of 190 or less out of 300):

Adaptive

Program resource adaptability: easily adapting to changes in program resources, including funding and staff

Leadership

Leadership sustainability: cultivating organizational leaders, avoiding an overreliance on one leader, and planning for leadership transition (including having a succession plan)

Technical

Marketing skills: ability to communicate effectively with internal and external stakeholders

Fundraising skills: ability to develop necessary resources for efficient operations, including management of donor relations

Source: TCC Group.

Decline

This chapter focuses on a phase of the lifecycle that is poorly understood: decline. The discussion will aim to help you understand previous writings and thoughts on nonprofit lifecycles and the decline phase, the trajectory of high-arc and low-arc organizations as they navigate the challenges and opportunities of this phase, the characteristics of organizations that are working through the decline phase, and strategies that can help declining nonprofits successfully navigate themselves through this phase.

As we think about organization development and groups that work with nonprofits in challenging circumstances, one organization that comes to mind is the Support Center of Nonprofit Management, a management support organization that has been serving New York City nonprofits for more than twenty years. For a number of years, the Support Center has been expanding its focus to look specifically at organizations in crisis. One of the key aspects of this work is its efforts in training longtime nonprofit consultants and practitioners as organizational turn-around specialists; the Support Center convenes this special group quarterly to discuss best practices, work through case studies, and share war stories. The war stories in this group often pertain to the boards and executive leadership that have made unfortunate decisions, or highlight cash-flow situations that point to an impending doom. The dialogue in these meetings often eventually moves to both the root cause of organizational crisis and a discussion of when the issues first began presenting themselves. Rarely could the group pinpoint exact times and places where organization crisis began, but all could point to multiple factors that played a role in deterioration during the downward trajectory. This is a very important point and one that will serve as an undercurrent throughout this chapter, as entering and being in the downward phase of the nonprofit lifecycle does not relate to just one organizational challenge but to a number of interconnected issues.

OVERVIEW OF DECLINE AND THE LIFECYCLE

In the Stevens lifecycle model, the downward phase is most commonly referred to as the decline phase, during which nonprofits typically experience the following challenges:

- Program participation has been reduced, and there are other programs in the marketplace that are both appealing to and relevant to the service community.
- As signs surface regarding organizational problems, leadership ignores the problems, denies them, or assigns blame to other places.
- The board of directors is disconnected from the challenges of the nonprofit until those challenges become much too big.
- The nonprofit's budget is not versatile and not well thought out, usually revisiting past efforts and not steeped in current realities.
- Organizational processes often steer the nonprofit into ineffective practices, and infrastructure severely limits the organization.

Stevens argues that during this phase, organizations make decisions based on internal interests rather than on an understanding of the needs of their program participants. As the organization declines, so too does its place in the market, significantly driving down both its demand and its revenue. Stevens believes that in this space, organizations become "self-aware" and use determination to reverse themselves through the lifecycle and into a more favorable position in the market, thus driving up revenue to become more supportive of their new status. According to Stevens, organizations in this phase typically engage in the following behaviors:

- A reassessment of programs occurs; in response to this assessment, programs are recast or realigned to more closely meet the needs of the market.
- An organizational leader grabs control of the organization, utilizing a variety of skills needed to move it through the crisis and into a healthier environment.

- A subsection of the committed board members reengages to help propel the organization to a better place.
- The organization utilizes a more realistic budget that shows a stronger relationship between expenses and income.
- Work might begin toward bringing organizational processes more in alignment with the needs of the changing organization.

HIGH-ARC AND LOW-ARC: HOW ORGANIZATIONS IN THE DECLINE PHASE ARE AFFECTED

The lifecycle model does not fully address the patterns and needs of the organization in the decline phase. As stated elsewhere in this book, the nonprofit lifecycle should not be viewed as a model that can be applied in the same way to all organizations. Although there might be somewhat reliable indicators of where an organization falls within the lifecycle, use of the model tends to be flawed, specifically when one is trying to understand organizations that are in the downward phase. For example, when we look at an organization that is more than fifty years old and has an annual operating budget of over $75 million, the downward phase might be quite different from that of a much smaller organization with a less-developed history. Would you apply the same board development techniques to the larger organization as you would to the smaller? Is the financial management different between the two? How agile is the larger and how advanced in its procedures, compared with the smaller group? Each organization's DNA is different and therefore requires a different strategy as it moves through the lifecycle. As discussed in the opening chapter, the high-arc/low-arc framework is helpful in addressing this discrepancy.

High-Arc Organizations—Decline Phase

High-arc organizations are those that experience a proportionately long period of growth and a short period during which they maintain the organization in a stable state. Essentially organizations grow to reach a state in which they can deliver a product that "works." For instance, an arts organization might find that it has established a firm footing in its community, has a consistent buying audience, has a stable facility in which to display its product, and is not necessarily looking to become larger. It just wants to continue to develop and refine the effort that it spent years growing into. In high-arc organizations, this period is often the shortest phase.

The high-arc organizational lifecycle is proportionately long in both the start-up or growth phase and in the downward phase. Whereas the middle part of a low-arc lifecycle can take a number of years, the high-arc organization's growth is often the longest period of time the organization spends on its lifecycle journey, especially if the organization is new and is going through the growth phase for the first time. As an example, the organization could be a microfinance group that has been inspired by the recent upsurge of focus on this area. Building on the public momentum of this cause, people become excited, programs are created and implemented, and resources and momentum are generated, all causing the organization to feel that the demand for its mission far exceeds the supply.

The downside of this growth might not be felt in a significant way for a long while. The work toward growth can often overtake all other functions. Some call this "growth for growth's sake," which is often accompanied by a tendency to pursue every funding opportunity without critically distinguishing appropriate opportunities from less relevant ones. Because of the initial high demand for the product, building internal infrastructure often takes a secondary role to the work of harnessing growth. The easy test to see where there are cracks in the organizational infrastructure is to look at whether the organization has job descriptions that fail to closely match the work actually being performed by staff, or whether financial management reports reflect current status but do not project a long-range financial direction. These two reflect only a few of a much larger number of infrastructural cracks that could be appearing. Bypassing these cracks, or "putting Band-Aids on bullet holes," is a fatal mistake that many organizations in fast or high growth commit. Overextending program growth and failing to appropriately attend to infrastructure are two key reasons that organizations experience a shortened maintain phase and a rapid and longer-term downward phase. Neglected infrastructure often exacerbates the challenges of the decline phase, causing this phase, along with growth, to dominate the organization's history. In traditional writings on the lifecycle, the maintain phase is the longest period in the organization's lifecycle, potentially lasting up to thirty years.

In order to reverse the downward trajectory, high-arc organizations in decline must focus on building specific areas of organizational capacity while also managing a downturn. Often many of these areas are addressed only when the organization is in crisis, but highly effective organizations look at them as part of their ongoing assessment process. The next paragraphs discuss three of these areas.

Cash Flow Management   In far too many nonprofits, the first time executives or boards see a cash flow statement is when cash flow becomes a serious issue. Getting an overview of an organization's cash position should not be an activity reserved only for organizations experiencing a cash crisis. Cash flow management is a function that takes time to master. Further, a time of crisis is not the ideal moment to be introduced to such a document or process. Organizations should establish use of a cash flow document as a normal part of financial reporting and certainly no later than when the leadership realizes that the organization is entering a downward phase. The Appendix includes a sample cash flow forecast summary, or cash flow statement, for an organization that is in a cash flow crisis (Table A.1). As the statement shows, the organization is experiencing a decline in revenue toward the end of the period, while the organizational expenses have remained relatively unchanged. In this simple example, one can see that maintaining expenses while revenues decline may cause a crisis if the nonprofit does not have reserves, which many do not.

Enhancing Board Bench Strength   When a board of directors finds itself in the midst of a downward trend, the members' roles and their connection to the organization are likely to shift. Board members may increase their involvement in day-to-day activities, or they may begin to move away from the organization as challenges grow, often because they lack the skill set that an organization requires if it is to weather a crisis.

Scenario Planning   As an organization starts to grapple with its challenges, it must also identify the structures and mechanisms its needs to regain and maintain stability. Within all phases of the lifecycle, movement occurs in stages; each stage is affected by the decisions made during the previous one. This is especially true of the downward phase. For example, say an organization decides to approach its closest funders in an attempt to obtain needed revenue to help it get through a difficult time. It has estimated that a certain amount of money will be obtained through this work. If it receives 50 percent less than planned, its next steps will be significantly altered in relation to the original plan. Scenario planning in a downward phase involves looking at the major actions that will be employed to address the crisis, then identifying the various contingencies that might follow from those actions, which will dictate the organization's next steps. Figure 5.1 is a simple example of a scenario planning tree.

Figure 5.1
Example of a Scenario Planning Tree

	1. Organization obtains 100% of goal in two months	1. Goal met, continue with traditional programs
		2. Goal met, redesign program structure for more effectiveness
	2. Organization obtains less than 100% but more than 75% of goal in two months	1. Cut programs with smaller numbers and funding bases
Organization has a major short-term deficit. Organization decides to approach key long-term donors.		2. Approach new tier of funders to obtain the remaining 25%
	3. Organization obtains less than 50% of goal in two months	1. Cut additional programs or shrink existing programs
		2. Approach new tier of funders to obtain the remaining 25%
	4. Organization obtains less than 25% of goal in two months	1. Cut majority of programs, holding on to flagship initiative
		2. Outside of additional funders, try alternative fundraising efforts

The Mind-Set of High-Arc Organizations in the Decline Phase

An organization that is deep in the decline phase may be suffering from many infrastructure challenges, but the most overwhelming is one that we might call "organizational self-esteem." The decline phase often hits the high-arc organization like the proverbial ton of bricks. Board members, community partners, and funders are often the most shocked at the infrastructure challenges because just a short time ago, the organization was in the midst of rapid growth and is still publicly regarded as a growth organization. The buffer between an organization in the growth phase and one in decline is the maintain phase. When that phase is short, it is common for the feelings associated with the growth phase to still be very present as the decline starts. These feelings at some point come into direct conflict with the realities of the decline phase, and organizational momentum begins to plummet. Like the infrastructure issues, momentum becomes a major challenge that the organization must overcome if it is to navigate this phase successfully.

Organizational self-esteem is not that different from individual self-esteem. According to leadership expert Mitch McCrimmon, people suffering from low self-esteem might exhibit the following characteristics and behaviors:[1]

- Feeling like a failure relative to everyone else and doubting they can achieve anything
- Playing it safe, not trying anything new
- Overly depending on others to look after them
- Escaping unpleasant realities
- Putting themselves down constantly

In the following paragraphs, we apply these characteristics to high-arc organizations in the decline phase and offer solutions that an organization can use, adopting a Tony Robbinsesque approach to dealing with low organizational self-esteem.

Feelings of failure and doubt. These are the immediate consequences of comprehending that the organization is in decline; they can easily become the dominant feelings within the organization.

Solution. Conducting a SWOT analysis or similar activity can be very valuable, allowing the organization to see how it looks in the present moment. The Appendix includes a SPOT analysis template (listing strengths, problems, opportunities, and threats), which can be used to build a common understanding of the organization's issues, remind itself of its strengths, and work out solutions.

Risk aversion. Its steep growth trajectory has caused the organization to be in the decline stage; the organization must change, but members may struggle to adopt new behaviors and practices. You might hear "This is the way things have always been done" uttered repeatedly as a comforting mantra justifying familiar activities, even if continuing as before is to the organization's detriment.

Solution. A time of crisis doesn't require the organization to take a radical turn in an opposite direction. If you're a community gardening organization, you don't need all of a sudden to become an association of scientists. "Curing" risk aversion is more about letting go and moving forward by identifying and changing the practices that have created the current problems. One of the best ways to identify more effective practices is to see how others are managing their organizations and performing and to adopt those practices that are effective and relevant. Organizational shadowing or mentoring is a great way to do this. Risk taking becomes less frightening if you've reduced the risk by adopting practices that organizations similar to yours have found effective.

- *Dependency.* Dependency relates directly to the organization's relationship to leadership. If the executive director (ED) or the board has been the dominant voice within the organization and its decisions have largely contributed to the organization's challenges, logic might lead one to think that a change in the dominant leadership is required. Instead, low self-esteem may cause the organization to cling to the challenged leadership structure; its dependency on that model clouds people's ability to take the necessary steps to make any change.

One example of this is commonly referred to as founder's syndrome, which occurs when the founder of an organization dominates nearly all aspects of the organization. During the founder's time with the organization, dependency on the executive is a major issue. One of the major points at which an organization might experience a sharp decline along the lifecycle is when its executive, especially a founder, leaves suddenly. The organization's dependence on the leader is showcased strongly when the organization falters in his or her absence. Another example is that of a strong board of directors that embeds itself in the day-to-day operations of the organization, especially in times of crisis, doing so to the potential detriment of staff buying into the direction of the organization laid out by the board. Both situations demonstrate the dependency of the organization on its leadership and relate to the organization not diversifying its leadership.

Solution. The solution to dependency is to diversify leadership. The Core Support Evaluation (CSE) tool we discussed in Chapter Four addresses the issue of diversifying both leadership and management approaches while concentrating tactics and perspectives on the most pressing and relevant issues facing the organization.

- *Reality aversion.* Reality aversion generally plays out in two different scenarios. In the first scenario, individuals within the organization are unknowingly avoiding the organization's current reality because they are generally unaware of the state of the organization. In this situation, there are multiple views of the organization's reality. In the second scenario, there is a common understanding of the organization's current challenges, but one or more of the individuals or parties do not subscribe to the current reality and operate according to some previous one. As we discussed earlier, many individuals within a high-arc organization in decline may not want to admit that the organization is in fact in decline, particularly when the time of organizational growth is still so fresh in their minds.

Solution. The solution to the "multiple views" type of reality aversion is to provide stakeholders with an objective assessment of the organization's challenges. (There are numerous tools for conducting this assessment, such as TCC Group's Core Capacity Assessment Tool [CCAT], information from which we have included in this chapter and in Chapters Two through Four; the Appendix also shows an example of a CCAT report [Figure A.2].) The results of an organizational assessment can give everyone involved a clear sense of the status of the organization and a perspective on its strengths and weaknesses. The second scenario is more difficult because stakeholders are apprised of the organization's challenges, but one or more parties disagree with the assessment and want to act counter to the necessary path for the nonprofit. The solution is to create avenues for dialogue and discussion. Through communication aimed at finding common ground on the current reality, the organization can move forward toward new realities.

- *Negativity.* In tough times, it is common for individuals to abandon the teamwork they may have experienced during growth and start blaming those who they feel are responsible for the current challenges. This causes the organization to shift its focus: instead of addressing the crucial structural issues, it begins concentrating on the emotional and relational issues. This in turn will only aggravate existing tensions and divert time and energy from the problems at hand.

Solution. Negativity can start among a small group of people and quickly become "viral." It is important that this negativity be addressed through an open process, that organizational values be reaffirmed, and that there be a framework that everyone must use to discuss their feelings and perceptions about what the organization's challenges are. The way to create this environment is to have a facilitated discussion of the values of the organization. Reaffirming shared beliefs and norms will create avenues of accountability and mechanisms to deal with the negativity before it derails recovery efforts.

Low-Arc Organizations—Decline Phase

The central difference between high-arc and low-arc organizations is in the duration of the MIE phase. As we discussed, for the high-arc organization, the MIE phase is frequently quite short. In low-arc organizations, it is typically much longer. Low-arc organizations are often much older and have probably moved through the lifecycle more than once and have thus gained an understanding of the benefits and challenges accompanying organizational growth.

Like high-arc organizations, low-arc organizations tend to be surprised when they find themselves in decline. Whereas high-arc organizations are surprised by the infrastructure issues that had never been addressed because of the brevity of the MIE phase, low-arc organizations are surprised by the sudden revelation that there has been a slow tearing of the infrastructure. The best example of this can be seen in program effectiveness. A low-arc organization may have a series of programs that it has delivered for a long period of time. Human service agencies with storied histories might have one or more signature programs that have been in their program mix for years. At the time of its creation, a program might have been unique, high impact, and innovative. As times and communities changed, perhaps the program became less relevant, or the evaluation criteria became stale, or the impact was reduced. Frequently an organization is delivering a program simply because the program has always been delivered. As this happens over time, competitive programs become more effective in meeting the needs of the same population, and the funding community shifts toward these higher-performing programs. The end result is that the organization's key programs have found themselves on the "outside looking in" as they relate to the funding community, and program participants have made the transition to the nonprofit with the more effective delivery system. Suppose that the organization's primary program historically represents approximately 40 percent of the budget; a shift by funders and the community might cause a 10 percent or more reduction in funding for this program and therefore present a major challenge to the future direction of that organization. For another example, if an organization has been receiving a certain portion of its funding to run an environmental program in a community affected by a polluting industry, and that industry then moves to another part of the world, the organization's environmental programming is likely to shift. Funding that it received before might be reduced, and therefore the organization will either need to adapt or find itself forced into a compromise.

A similar challenge can apply to a low-arc organization's board of directors. As anyone who has visited a number of board-of-directors meetings would note, they are often steeped in ritual. Adhering to these rituals can be bad for a board: members may be blinded to new challenges to the organization. In this type of organization, you might see members who have been on the board for over ten or twenty years. They may sit in the same seating arrangements; certain people deliver the same messages; and the agenda for one meeting is exactly the same as that of another, with only the date changed. In the same way that certain program activities are performed because they have always been performed, board members fit into patterns that are replicated at every board meeting. Bob is the financial expert, Jean is the individual with direct experience in the nonprofit's program areas, and they will perform these roles in the play called *Board of Directors*. As the programs begin to tear and the board continues to perform the same play, the gap between the product and the governing structure widens. The long period that is the maintain phase for the low-arc organization often causes the board of directors to become very far removed from the real day-to-day work of the organization, which in turn affects its ability both to obtain resources and to advocate publically for the organization. A far-removed board of directors can be harmful to an organization in the decline phase, having a significant negative impact on future funding and playing a frayed role in guiding the organizational leader.

The prime advantage that a low-arc organization has over a high-arc one is that low-arc organizations have time to make adjustments to their trajectory, whereas high-arc organizations are reacting to a steep decline. Where high-arc organizations experience low self-esteem, low-arc organizations tend to be complacent. The following are some characteristics of organizational complacency, along with solutions relating to each characteristic:

- *Trusting to a fault.* Trust is at the base of routine. Using the same hairstylist or buying fruit from the same farmers' market for years is an example of how routine filters into our daily lives. We trust that we will receive a good haircut or fresh fruit each time we visit. The same kind of trust can develop toward leadership in the organization. Because the organization looks and feels the same each and every day, over time everyone comes to trust that the organization will look and feel the same tomorrow. This blind trust can have a lasting negative impact on the organization because it remains in place even while outside the organization there are a variety of factors changing every day, including philanthropy, community needs, and socioeconomic demographics. Blind trust can also be a symptom of a larger leadership issue, at both the board and ED levels.

Solution. If an executive can get to the point where she can trust the various areas of an organization to function effectively without involving herself directly in every detail, that is a sign of healthy trust; she in turn is more likely to be trusted by the people working in those areas. Essentially, the engine has been built, and now the organization can drive. However, every once in a while you have to take the car in for diagnostics. Low-arc organizations should create some kind of mechanism that helps ensure that the organization is functioning well, an internal audit that monitors a variety of areas.

• *"It ain't broke."* If some people get the impulse to tinker under the hood and fix certain areas within a low-arc organization, others will push back, arguing "If it ain't broke, don't fix it." There are two problems with this notion. The first is that adherents of this viewpoint assume that the organization must be in a much more dire position before the organization should "fix it," essentially advocating for the organization to be nearly broke financially or broken structurally before taking action. The second problem, which is more cultural, is that the leadership has taken a position of not dealing with issues as they arise. All levels of leadership must deal with organizational issues, and tabling these efforts limits leaders' ability to address challenges. The ability to deal with organizational challenges is a muscle that needs to be worked out, or it will wither.

Solution. This attitude can almost be equated to a disease or syndrome. The symptoms include consistently repeating the same patterns and blocking new ideas or attempts to alter these patterns. The solution to this problem is to break up the process that dictates the patterns. If board members sit in the same seats at board meetings or flow through the same agenda patterns, then create a standing policy that board meetings will have features that change with each meeting—for example, an issue speaker or a client presentation. Change the meeting location. If an executive comes in each morning and immediately goes to the office to pour through e-mails, have her step out of the office each day and spend some time walking through the programs and visiting with staff. The walk-through can change the executive's perspective and her approach to her work.

• *Macro, macro, and more macro.* Numerous books, management schools, and leadership theories encourage leaders to enhance their ability to look at their organization at the macro level. Accordingly, organizational leaders often believe that viewing the organization as a whole rather than attending to its many parts is the ideal perspective. Regardless of theory, adopting a macro-level overview dissuades leaders from expending the time and energy necessary to conduct a micro-level analysis of the state of the organization. Board members also fall victim to this tendency to focus just on the macro, believing that taking a micro-level view might mean that they are involving themselves too closely in the day-to-day work, or that they don't have opportunities to take a micro-level view.

Solution. When a low-arc organization realizes that it is beyond the maintain phase and is in decline, the worry of many executives is the reaction of the board. A board may immediately become more hands-on—or it may decide to be more hands-off. Achieving the right level of involvement becomes the work of both the board and the executive. One of the signs that a low-arc organization is in the decline phase is that there has been a gradual peeling off of board members. The organization is different now than it was in the beginning, but board members' roles have become stagnant. Departing board members are often replaced with exact replicas: "We lost a zookeeper, so we need to find another zookeeper to fill the gap."

This is a flawed strategy and misses an opportunity at a critical time to gain the board member whom the organization truly needs. The board member you needed in the growth phase is much different from the one you need in decline; for example, having someone who is a special-event expert might not be as relevant now; someone who is an expert in human resources or real estate financing might be more beneficial in the current situation. A board matrix is a commonly used tool for gaining understanding of what the organization's board needs in relation to what the board currently has in terms of members' skills and resources. One means of moving from an entirely macro perspective on the board is to change the board roles, creating new member roles that look closely at the specific areas that are most pertinent to the organization in the decline phase. The board should be an amoeba-like entity, changing to best meet the needs of the organization.

• *Dwindling passion for the mission.* One of the main differences between growing organizations and those that are in the decline phase is that nonprofits in the growth stage often exhibit a high level of energy around their mission. This passion is the main reason these nonprofits are growing—the momentum and excitement keep partners, staff, and funders engaged. In contrast, if you are sitting in a board meeting or walking into the lobby of a nonprofit in the end of the MIE phase or as it enters decline, you would never suspect that the organization is geared toward a specific mission. There is minimal excitement, and you might feel that the organization is merely going through the motions. The loss of energy around the mission, or the perception that energy has been lost, poses a variety of potential challenges to the organization, including a negative impact on staff morale and negative interactions with partners and clients.

Solution. A common statement that one might hear from ground-level staff during a crisis is that the board and the executives don't care about the work of the organization. Attend a board meeting during times of decline and ask individual board members what the organization is doing on the ground; if it is an eleven-member board, you will probably get eleven different responses. The problem here is not really one of passion, but one of connection—a connection to the work, a connection to the staff, and a connection to the mission.

The disconnect can be repaired by reengaging those who have become dispassionate and providing opportunities for them to reconnect and to develop relationships with those who are probably mischaracterizing them. During times of crisis or decline, the solution to the passion challenge is to shrink the space between those on the front line and those at the executive and board levels to show everyone that there is a common affinity for the mission. A good example of this could be intertwining board engagements with an aspect of the program or having a refresher meeting with board members to align roles with their current passions. A board member who was interested in marketing when he came aboard might over time develop an interest in finance but not have had an opportunity to apply that interest. This may just be the time to make a change.

THE ARC DURING CRISIS

In September of 2008, the United States began to experience a very serious economic crisis. This economic downturn had a profound effect on the nonprofit and philanthropic landscapes. Philanthropic giving has shifted, foundations have reprioritized, and government contracting has become more burdensome. This has caused serious financial challenges for a majority of nonprofit organizations. This has also changed the arc of nonprofit organizations, especially those approaching the decline phase. Ordinarily, an organization can be in the decline phase anywhere from three to ten years. During tough economic times, because of the aforementioned challenges and others, this time frame may be shortened significantly, for reasons we outline here. We also offer some solutions.

- *Revenue loss.* When the economy demands that a funder change its giving strategy, it often has to make very difficult decisions that can have a sweeping impact on a nonprofit organization. Similarly, when a government agency, many times a state agency, is forced to alter its payment structure or reduce payments on its contracts, its actions can have a huge negative impact on the organizations with which the agency works. These revenue challenges can force organizations to confront tough financial decisions, and if cash flow is threatened, decisions often reserved for the turnaround phase are forced to be discussed much earlier. In times of economic crisis, low-arc organizations may have a steeper arc, and high-arc organizations have an arc that looks more like a cliff.

In looking at an organization's cash flow, one of the areas in which significant resources are allocated is payroll. In fact, the majority of organizational expenses go toward human capital. Although staffing cuts are to be expected during times of financial crisis, the staffing allocations should also be revisited to see if there might be flexibility in the budget lines that could be considered to help alleviate the need for future cuts. For example, administrative and technical staff are often left out of the program staffing mix when in fact these staff members do spend their time working directly on behalf of the programs. Nonprofits working with a government contract may try to shift the contract to include these staff members.

• *Board readiness.* As discussed earlier, boards in low-arc organizations that are approaching or are in decline may have neither the skill set nor the makeup to effectively handle a decline, especially one that is more rapid due to the economic crisis. Essentially, the board got out of shape during the maintain phase and now is being asked to compete in the 400-meter sprint. This is just not going to go well. The board needs to be a real asset in helping the organization navigate a steepened decline phase, but it is often left flat-footed.

A potential solution to this problem might be to conduct a board reorientation that reacquaints board members with the state of the organization and what their role or responsibility needs to be to help the organization in this new economic climate. If a strategic plan exists for the organization, hold a working session that revisits the assumptions laid out in the strategic plan; discuss the new assumptions and realities that exist and decide how the strategic plan should be operationalized in light of this new view.

• *Staff readiness.* Staff may not have become complacent during the maintain phase; nevertheless, the way they went about their work during that phase is much different than it is during the decline phase. The sudden movement into the decline phase can bring a great deal of confusion for staff, particularly when the organization is perceived as vulnerable. Where staff members were once talking about program efforts, they are now talking about staff cuts. This sudden shift in circumstances can damage staff morale and reduce their trust in the leadership; it also requires changes in roles and adjustments to adapt to limited resources.

The solution for the organization in decline is to engage both staff and board in a process that discusses how the work must change. Because often the majority of staff have not been involved in some of the top-level discussions, leaders should create an open space where staff can discuss their current feelings about the organization and have an opportunity to offer feedback about its future. The organization needs to develop a short-term, detailed plan that honestly addresses the most urgent problems. Most important is that stakeholders challenge each other to make mission and impact the highest priority. It is essential to engage funders or community partners in this process as well. Often nonprofits and their external stakeholders do not engage in honest dialogue because doing so might jeopardize reputation, funding, or both. In failing to engage, organizations miss important opportunities for learning best practices, gaining new information, and acquiring valuable mentors. In the case of community partners, open dialogue may also lead to opportunities for resource sharing and collaboration.

• *Mission impact.* If you're a doctor and you're going into surgery, you would assume that the surgery table has all the tools necessary for you to perform that surgery. Now imagine taking away the scalpel or the EKG machine. Can you do the work as effectively? In ordinary circumstances, there are reductions in the available tools over the course of a shift from the maintain phase to the decline phase; when an economic crisis is thrown on top of the decline phase, the tools that an organization has available to achieve its mission are reduced even more.

In a related challenge, an organization may have access to tools and resources and not use them. For instance, imagine that you ship the operating room at the Mayo Clinic to a less resourced hospital. The doctors in the less-resourced community may be amazed at the resources that are now available, but they ultimately will work with their own tools because they have been able to successfully meet the needs of their patients with these tools; they may adjust only slightly with the addition of the new tools. These medical examples show that organizations should be thinking not about achieving less impact during tough times but about recalibrating the way in which the work is conducted to achieve the same level of impact and potentially achieving even greater impact. For example, many organizations are smartly looking at their volunteer management effort and realizing that they have underutilized volunteers and pro bono help; having done that, they can reconfigure their volunteer programs and invest in those who are freely giving their time.

• *Funder and partner relationships.* When guests are scheduled to come and visit, it's a common practice for the hosts to clean up the house to give the impression that the house always looks immaculate. Organizations in the decline phase tend to do the same. When a funder conducts a site visit, many nonprofits put on their "Sunday best"; staff members may stand a little straighter, hallways look a little cleaner, and programs look a little crisper. The discussion of an organization's challenges becomes a risky proposition: funding might be lost. This situation is not created entirely by the nonprofit. In fact, it has been created by funders, who often punish nonprofits that engage in real dialogue. The same holds true when nonprofits meet with community partners, not only in terms of retaining funding but also because the organization must maintain an impression that it is strong and that "all is well." The inability of organizations to engage in a peer-to-peer dialogue on organizational challenges cuts out important best-practice exchanges and opportunities for mentorship. Further, as funders are "hubs" for many like-minded organizations, they are often missing the opportunity to engage organizations in real peer-to-peer learning.

Solutions to this issue are numerous, but one of the main solutions is to allow partners and funders into the conversation about successfully pulling through this tough economic situation. With regard to partners, organizations should outline all the resources of partner organizations to help discover potential resource gaps and how the partners might be able to assist in meeting each other's needs. For example, one partner might identify a real need in technology staffing; the other might suggest that it has a great full-time technology manager who has time that could be dedicated to the needs of the partner. The partners could essentially share both the costs and the benefits of this previously underutilized technology staff member.

There is much discussion of the resources that funders have outside of financial resources. One of their resources is their access to information. Suppose a funder receives a couple dozen midyear reports on the progress and results of their grantees; it is possible that this information would be of interest to other like-minded organizations. Foundations could develop a mechanism for sharing this information while also facilitating dialogue among their grantees on best practices and approaches to tough economic times. Funders can be excellent "matchmakers" for organizations looking for new approaches to their work.

DECLINE PHASE INTERVIEW

The following is an interview with Thomas Wolf, a leading expert on organization development. His book *And the Band Stopped Playing: The Rise and Fall of the San Jose Symphony* relates closely to the content of this chapter. Wolf's career spans more than four decades and encompasses the fields of philanthropy, education, and the arts. He established the Cambridge office of WolfBrown in 1983 after serving as the founding director of the New England Foundation for the Arts for seven years. His clients have included ten of the fifty largest U.S. foundations; such government agencies as the National Endowment for the Arts; and treasured international cultural institutions such as the British Museum, the Boston Symphony Orchestra, and the Kennedy Center. Wolf has consulted directly with the leaders of major cities, including Chicago, Cleveland, Charlotte, Los Angeles, Phoenix, Philadelphia, and Dallas, on the creation of vibrant cultural communities. His workshops and convocations for trustees, administrators, and volunteers have earned him national recognition.

Wolf holds a doctorate in education from Harvard and has taught at Harvard and Boston Universities. He is the author of *The Search for Shining Eyes: Audiences, Leadership and Change in the Symphony Orchestra Field*; *Managing a Nonprofit Organization in the 21st Century*; and *Presenting Performances in the 21st Century*, among numerous articles and books. A professional flutist, he is listed in *The International Who's Who of Music*. The following outlines his thoughts on the decline phase.

As you think about organizations in the decline phase, what are the characteristics of an organization that successfully navigates decline and what are those of groups that have trouble moving through decline?

The greatest challenge is to find leaders who are clear-eyed about assessing the realities of their organization's situation. This means shedding any nostalgia about history and tradition and rather analyzing what the future is likely to be. It involves determining whether the mission is still relevant, whether the organization is well suited to carrying out that mission, whether others are doing it better, what the funding base looks like, whether the volunteer and staff leadership is up to the task of carrying things forward. Often outside consulting help can be critical to securing a truly objective sense of the organization's current reality and future, especially since there will be people on both sides of the issue internally (those who want continuation, those who want dissolution) who either do not want to hear a grim prognosis or want to exaggerate one. The key is having leaders who can focus the board on a commonsense view of where things stand and bring them to a moment where they recognize the inevitable. It is nice to have a scenario that not only resolves the situation, but also provides some sense of accomplishment (for example, another organization can take over existing programs) or eases the pain (finding alternate employment for staff).

As you think about groups that have entered the decline phase, what are the skills leaders and boards need in tough times?

Leaders must be objective, willing to accept realities, and able to deliver news that many people do not want to hear. But this is a delicate balancing act. On the one hand, they cannot sugarcoat the information. On the other, there may be situations where the bad news, judiciously presented along with a series of options, can produce donors who will lead the organization to stability and sustainability. I once consulted for an orchestra that was in decline and that clearly could not afford to operate according to the mode they had chosen—as a full-time professional unionized organization. After presenting three scenarios to the board, one of the trustees asked, "How much would it take to provide sufficient endowment to operate the way you have proposed in your most optimistic scenario?" Having done an analysis of earned and contributed income potential, I said, "$35 million." His answer was, "I will provide half if the community will match it." Had the leader of the board not been open to presenting alternatives, this lifesaving gesture would never have occurred.

Getting out of a decline takes a variety of organizational skills; which of these skills are the most pivotal?

One of the key moves an organization has to make to get out of decline is to empower a small group to begin the essential diagnostic work that will lead to recommendations on restructuring, dissolution, or anything else. Sometimes this process is done openly—the chairman appoints a group or the executive committee takes it on—and on the surface, one would think this is always the best way to proceed. But that is not necessarily the case. I have seen situations where the issues are so fraught with challenges that a small group (always led by the chair or president) begins the diagnostic work quietly, often utilizing the services of a consultant. In one case, a group was concerned that its founder-director would begin to lobby board members; in another, people believed that staff would hear rumors and start leaving at a critical moment; in a third, there was worry that foundations would get wind of the process and would hold back funding. Ultimately, once the diagnosis has been completed, an open process of education and debate must take place. But it is best done only after the facts have been assembled. Whatever occurs—an open discussion process or a secret diagnostic one—one individual, and one individual only, should serve as spokesperson, and strong insistence should be made that all questions (especially from the media) be directed to that individual.

What is important to know and understand about decline when a group is in start-up or growth? Are there things a nonprofit should think about long before a potential decline can occur?

Every group should understand that the world changes, and unless organizations change and adapt, they will decline and eventually go out of business. This is why strategic planning on a regular basis is so important. Good planning begins with some kind of environmental scan and organizational assessment. The classic SWOT analysis (strengths, weaknesses, opportunities, threats) has been refined often over the years, but it is still the essential tool for monitoring how organizations are doing and how they need to reposition themselves in terms of new realities. New groups often feel they have the franchise on new ideas, but they need to be reminded that someday they will be old groups, and their thinking may be just as stale as those they are currently replacing. It is absolutely essential, therefore, to make serious planning—with outside objective assessment—part of an organization's culture from day one.

As you think about the nonprofit sector today, what are areas of innovation that nonprofits can think of in light of the challenges presented by the current economy, the impending leadership gap caused by the retiring of baby boomers, and the current funding environment?

In the current environment, there are several areas on which nonprofits need to focus:

First, they need to look for opportunities for collaboration, strategic alliances, and even mergers. Most nonprofit sectors are overbuilt, and there is redundancy in program delivery. There is also a limited resource base. Successful organizations are ones that are finding ways to be more efficient by sharing resources, coming up with combined administrative structures, cooperating on programming, and looking for resources together.

Second, they need to understand the implication of new technology, especially in the area of communication and marketing. The younger generation does not rely anymore on traditional media, and the way they get their information requires a new understanding of the nature of shared experience and viral communication. This area changes so quickly that it is difficult for organizations to keep up. Being one technological generation behind the curve (which often means a year or less) helps sort out the short-term trends from real change.

Third, leaders of organizations must be able to articulate their missions and priorities in terms of community needs and in the language of broad community goals. They need to talk about their work in terms of economic development, public safety, community wellness, twenty-first-century workforce development, the environment, and so on. The impact of their work needs to be broadly understood by local citizens who are not necessarily interested in the specifics of their activities or operations. But if these activities are meeting community challenges (or at least are described that way), there is greater traction with a broad public.

They need to focus on monitoring indicators of financial sustainability—proper capitalization, financial stability, funding—as well as general organizational sustainability: strong leadership, proper management, and general relevance to twenty-first-century needs. Building strong, sustainable organizations is neither new nor necessarily innovative, but the ways this is being done successfully in an era of shrinking resources, greater public accountability, and increased competition involve much innovative thinking.

chapter SIX

Turnaround and Closing

This chapter focuses on the turnaround phase, one that many nonprofits see only as a challenging time during their lives and that others regard much more seriously. It's understandable why many practitioners might feel this way, as turnaround can often mean that the organization is tasked with doing a great deal of organizational change with very few resources. There is an upside to the turnaround phase, though, in that it can represent the "rebirth" of an organization.

Organizational turnaround and the closing of an organization are the least written about areas of thought and research relating to the nonprofit lifecycle, even though they are a driving force behind what occurs in other phases of the lifecycle. For example, successful organizations in the decline phase can work toward restoring impact by both cutting out excesses and building capacity; thus, should they decide to turn around, they have a stronger foundation from which to work. In doing this, an organization always has its eye on two future competing options: turning around or closing. As part of a turnaround, the organization also can consider creating a merger or a strategic alliance.

In this chapter, we discuss the characteristics of organizations that find themselves in this phase; the trajectory of high-arc and low-arc organizations as they work through the turnaround phase, and the challenges associated with each type; and strategies that can help organizations successfully navigate through this phase of the lifecycle. We also include a case study of a Brooklyn organization that approached the turnaround phase and made an important organizational choice.

HISTORICAL LOOK AT LIFECYCLE THOUGHT: CLOSING

As is true of businesses, many nonprofit organizations close down within a few years of opening. The starting of these organizations is usually a great idea and involves a burst of energy that quickly fizzles after the realization of the long-term burdens of operating a nonprofit organization sets in. In Judith Sharken Simon's *Five Life Stages of Nonprofit Organizations*, the final stage is called the "review and renew" stage and works under the assumption that a nonprofit should and will move to revitalizing its effort.[1] Simon addresses "decline and dissolution" through an organization's performance in a checklist on several organizational areas. The "closing" area is not part of the lifecycle but more of a chute for organizations that are no longer viable.

Stevens outlines all the characteristics of organizations in the decline phase, identifying the challenges they face. Although the basic arc of the lifecycle remains the same, the Stevens model allows for differential classification of individual organizational areas. For example, an organization might be in the growth phase relating to its programs but in the decline phase relating to governance. Nevertheless, a final lifecycle determination is likely to be similar throughout the various categories, especially when one is looking at an organization in the closing phase. For example, during the decline or closing phase, it is unlikely that an organization's programs would be in growth but its infrastructure in decline. If an organization is in decline, it is more than likely that a majority of its subareas are also in decline.

The overall weakness in both Simon's view and the Stevens model is that they assume that the arc of the lifecycle is the same for every organization, as if the trajectory for each nonprofit were the same. For example, imagine a large human services organization with a more than hundred-year history. It finds itself in financial distress comparable to that of an organization that is seven years old and that grew very rapidly, has little infrastructure, and has seen some funders pull away in the midst of an economic crisis. Do these organizations experience decline or turnaround in the same way and progress through the phase at the same rate? Probably not. Decline and turnaround for the younger organization will be much faster because it is a higher-arc organization compared to the human services organization, which is probably a low-arc organization and probably has more time to see the coming closing phase. High-arc and low-arc organizations are going to employ different approaches and make different decisions about closing, for although they are both in the same phase of the lifecycle, they are nevertheless in different positions.

THE DOWNWARD APEX POINT

As nonprofits decline, they naturally approach a point when they ask the question, *Should we close down, or should we try to turn this thing around?* If the organization is a high-arc organization whose decline has been more rapid, the need for a decision may arise more quickly than anticipated. The point at which this decision is made is known as the "downward apex point," or DAP (see Figure 6.1). Organizations at the DAP can choose to do one of three things. The first is to form a strategic alliance with another organization, often referred to as a merge. The second and most popular is the organizational turnaround; this can take many different forms, but the common element of a successful turnaround is that all involved agree to a significant change in their organizational DNA. The third option is for the organization to decide to close or "sunset," essentially ending the organization's efforts to fulfill its mission.

Being at the DAP only occurs when the organization realizes that it has few options with regard to its future. Low-arc organizations, which have moved at a slower pace toward the DAP, may have more time to deliberate on their future decisions. High-arc organizations, which are likely to have been moving through the decline phase more rapidly, may have less time for deliberation and less information with which to make their decisions.

As we mentioned, most organizations opt for turnaround. High-arc organizations that have less time to deliberate may make the wrong decisions when opting for turnaround, causing an eventual, though often immediate, organizational closing.

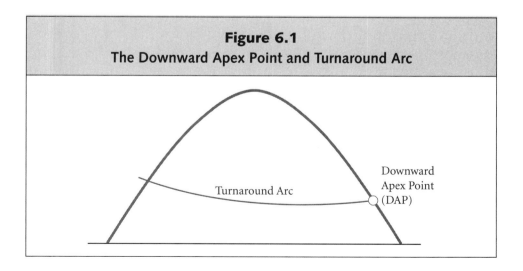

Figure 6.1
The Downward Apex Point and Turnaround Arc

Turnaround Arc

Downward
Apex Point
(DAP)

For organizations that do not approach the turnaround phase strategically, or for those that should have decided on another option, turnaround has a limited chance of succeeding; these organizations are taking a "Hail Mary" approach to turning themselves around. Organizations that make the decision to turn around after entertaining the option of either entering a strategic alliance or closing down may also be throwing a Hail Mary when entering the turnaround phase because of the time lost in pursuing the other endeavors.

ORGANIZATIONAL TURNAROUND

Several years ago, we were approached about helping an organization in the decline phase. The organization, let's call it Main Street Services (MSS), had lost its largest government contract to another competitor and had to move its operational home to the back of its thrift store. Program services were marginal, and its remaining funding sources came from the thrift store and some small individual donations from the community. The twenty-year-old organization, which had a budget of just over a million dollars, had seen a steady and rapid descent through the decline phase; approaching the DAP, the board had decided to turn the organization around and was looking for an organizational change expert to help. In this section we will follow this case study through the turnaround experience while also highlighting the differences in turnaround between high-arc organizations (as in the case study) and low-arc organizations. The case study will follow the turnaround phase in three distinct sections of the turnaround arc:

1. Assessment and market analysis
2. Shifting of organizational "DNA"
3. Growth readiness

Assessment and Market Analysis

When an organization makes a decision to turn around, the question becomes, *What are we turning around to?* To answer that question, the organization must begin a period of "looking under the hood," looking inward and assessing all aspects of the organization. This assessment should look at all available information, but certain information is important to inspect very early on because these data can help answer the additional questions that will arise, further fueling the assessment process. For example, a look into program effectiveness and impact might showcase that certain staff roles are heavily concentrated in one area as compared with another, thus bringing up a potential human resource issue. The following are areas to investigate as part of a thorough assessment:

- Financial infrastructure and performance
- Program effectiveness and impact
- Resource development infrastructure and results
- Board development infrastructure and planning
- Administrative and operational systems design and implementation

It is important to note that these assessment areas are relevant to any assessment in the life of a nonprofit. The difference in the assessment of a turnaround organization is that the areas that are found to be weak are areas that will be shed entirely, and the strong areas may serve as the core of what the new organization becomes when it leaves the turnaround phase. For example, an organization that finds a number of smaller programs ineffective and expensive is more likely to discard these efforts as it turns around, whereas the same organization during the growth phase might have simply readjusted the efforts to align more closely with its growth. Simply put, the purpose of assessment in the turnaround phase is to determine which areas will be discarded.

In addition to looking inward, the organization will also need to look outward and conduct a market analysis to assess trends that are shaping demand for its programs and services. These include demographic shifts, trends in public and private funding, public opinion, and the policy environment. For example, a nonprofit dedicated to low-income youth might realize that socioeconomic conditions have changed within the community over time or that the number of organizations serving the same mission area has increased in the community. The analysis should also look at related service areas to see if there are important community challenges that are not being focused on specifically. Another important target for study is whatever is considered to be "best practice" in the specific field or subsector.

Layering the outward analysis on top of the internal analysis should allow the organization to better understand its capacities and challenges and where it should aim to shift its focus to have impact.

Case Study: As we noted earlier, Main Street Services hired us to help it through several major challenges and onto a path to becoming a renewed organization. This work began with a deep assessment of the internal and external strengths and weaknesses of the organization and an assessment of community needs as they related to services for homeless children and families. The assessment of MSS found some of the following challenges and opportunities:

Internal Challenges

- MSS had provided services in the same manner for more than twenty years, although the homeless population had changed considerably during that time. In order to move forward, the nonprofit needed to recalibrate its work to serve the homeless and low-income individuals and families in new and more innovative ways.

- The board of directors had been very involved in the day-to-day operations of the organization, but did not involve itself in the development of resources or partnerships for the organization. Board members had never set goals or been given any orientation. Brand-new board mechanisms and systems would need to be created for the addition of new board members and to create a strategy for growth. In addition, the board would need to consider what skills and abilities were missing from the previous board membership and think about realigning its makeup to meet its future needs.

- The organizational systems and infrastructure were severely strained: organizational information was housed in several locations, and the main office was using outdated computer systems. MSS would need to create brand-new administrative and IT infrastructures that would support a future renewed organization.

External Opportunities

- MSS's geographic community was located in the fastest-growing region in the United States, and homelessness and poverty were growing at an equal rate. The main challenge was that a majority of the general public had no knowledge or understanding of the growth in the number of homeless. MSS had the opportunity to educate and engage new partners and donors and create new funding streams to support the organization.

- A majority of the homeless organizations in the community were not altering their approach to serving the homeless, including measuring their quality or effectiveness. MSS had an opportunity to look at current best practices and formulate a new model. MSS, like other organizations, had to this point only counted the number of people in its care, rather than looking at how the services provided would help homeless people find permanent self-sufficiency. By developing and finalizing a model that would work toward this goal, the organization had an additional opportunity to create metrics to measure elements of the new model, which would allow it to adjust to increase impact as needed.

- MSS did not have an effective method for recruiting volunteers or steering them into roles in which they could make meaningful contributions and feel valued. By redesigning a volunteer program that utilized the assets of community members, the organization had a chance to bring in new constituents to the mission of the organization while also enabling experienced community members to address unmet needs.

Although MSS did not do any assessment or community scan early in the process, through a much-needed organizational assessment and community scan much later, MSS was able to begin movement along the turnaround arc and think about a renewal of the organization.

Shifting of Organizational "DNA"

Now that the organization has a fuller understanding of its opportunities and challenges, it must begin the transformation from an organization on the decline to one in a growth phase, based on an organizational model that is much different. This process is not unlike adaptation in nature; as Darwin discusses in his work in evolution, for a species to survive it must change or adjust in response to changes in its environment. Similarly, organizations must adapt if they are going to turn themselves around and enter a new phase of the nonprofit lifecycle. Organizations that are not able to adapt must choose to close or find the opportunity to formally align with another effort. Organizations that decide to turn themselves around must go through significant changes that will help them emerge from the turnaround stage as a transformed organization poised to achieve impact.

Following the assessment, an organization can start on a path similar to that undertaken by an individual seeking to make a life change. The connection between human development and organization development, especially when looking at a turnaround, is remarkably close. A search of books on Amazon.com using the key words "stages of life" yields more than ten thousand titles. One of the more popular books of recent years is *Becoming a Life Change Artist,* by Fred Mandell and Kathleen Jordan.[2] Their model outlines several change techniques that the most creative minds in history shared and practiced in their life turnarounds; these techniques closely resemble the changes necessary for an organization that is changing its organizational DNA. The following are the stages of organizational change, again using the case study to illustrate them.

Preparing   An organization that starts a turnaround must prepare itself for this effort. After the internal and community assessments, the organization must use these data to confront the challenges within the organization and the dynamics of an ever-changing community. Many organizations have real difficulty with this first stage because they want to enter the turnaround process retaining many of the same actors and structures that caused the problems in the decline phase. Changing an organization's DNA means making fundamental changes in the structure, or skeleton, of the organization. Board members must change because turnaround requires a different type of board member skill set. Programs must be aimed toward new outcomes. A new staffing structure must be aligned to meet a new delivery of services. The organizational analysis and community assessment should help point the organization in the right direction, but the organization must begin to move forward. Although each nonprofit, and thus each turnaround process, is unique, there are some common themes that most organizations in the turnaround phase will share, the most immediately critical being "Get the right people on the bus," as Jim Collins might say in his book *Good to Great.* As in the start-up phase, the number of people on the board will be small but focused, a team of real specialists. Having board members with specific skills in program development, community affairs, organization development, and fund development might prove invaluable. The previous board may have moved like an institutional board, but this board is a working board.

Staff is probably reduced due to the revenue challenges that declining organizations typically face, so staff realignment is important. Having individuals who are able to transition across multiple program areas is key. Whereas board members will have to be specialists, it is best for staff members to be generalists who can move across multiple organizational areas.

Like staff, the program mix might shrink considerably. The programs may not be the ones that the organization ultimately offers once the turnaround is complete. If there are specialized services, such as ESL classes, that are popular, then the community assessment should show that these services can be expanded upon. If the services are general programming, such as afterschool activities or information and referral, then the organization may need to specialize aspects of the program and narrow the focus.

Case Study: MSS had been experiencing several years of decline, having faced a difficult relationship with a previous long-term funder and still working itself out from under the large shadow of the founder. When the organization lost a primary funder, it started to realize that it was really struggling and that it needed to turn the organization around or end up closing. The organization did not conduct a formal assessment and used the challenging feedback from its funders to hire a new leader who could help it through the hard times. The organization made successful strides toward turnaround, but a formal assessment would have helped it more effectively address unseen issues such as board development and organizational infrastructure issues. The organization had to address these issues much later, which interfered with its turnaround process.

Seeing New Perspectives   Once the organization can see beyond the past and organize itself accordingly, it must now start to see what it can become. This is an important step because it can generate a great deal of excitement during a period when it is likely that no one has been feeling particularly excited. The last couple of months and years have probably been difficult, and the organization is still watching its cash flow closely, but now there is the discussion of "what can be." During this time, it is important to observe closely what the community assessment data are saying. Are there more young people in the community? More seniors? Are there increasing environmental concerns? Is there a gap in your arts and cultural offerings? The goal is to determine how your organization could adapt so as to address the challenges or gaps revealed by the community needs assessment. When considering adaptation, it is important not to aim to become an organization that is completely different from your former self. Change should be organic, not artificial. Snakes do not evolve into polar bears. A community gardening project can expand enough to educate young people about the environment or advocate on behalf of healthy lifestyles, which is on the outside of its direct mission. If, however, the community garden ventures into providing health services—making a major identity change rather than a structural one—this will only confuse the community and potential supporters. More important, such a change would not be a natural expansion of what the nonprofit already does well; such dramatic change might in fact be perpetuation of bad habits, by which opportunities were chosen without considering their relation to the overall strategy of the organization.

To begin a strategic discussion on its potential new direction, the organization will need to see the world differently. In most nonprofits, the only frame of reference the board has is the organization that it serves; boards rarely have speakers come to talk about advances in the field respective to their missions. During a turnaround, such "consciousness raising" is not just a nice thing to do: it is mandatory. Fieldwork is important because the organization is beginning to create a frame of reference for its future. Once they have conducted some brainstorming via the community assessment research, board members and staff should investigate organizations that have been regarded as top performers in this area or organizations in the general region that are performing in this service area.

Case Study: As MSS began thinking about its future, it looked at the work of other homeless organizations within the region and also at joining regional and national homeless networks that it had previously avoided. Much work was being done among these groups to find more beds for the growing homeless population, and MSS began having executives from these networks come and engage in individual discussions with the board and staff.

The organization decided that this approach was flawed and that there would never be enough beds for everyone. Additional ancillary services would need to be created to meet the needs of this growing population. As the organization began to think about its future direction, it investigated other national service models, including drop-in homeless facilities and specialized shelters, and began to think about specific program areas in the homeless service community that it could recommit to.

Embracing Uncertainty and Taking Risks   Once the organization has decided to begin turnaround, it must now begin entering the new "space" it will occupy as a changed effort. This is the most critical stage in the turnaround phase because it is the time in which an organization firmly commits to a new direction. This can be both a very exciting and a very scary time—exciting because the organization is starting to see new areas to explore and motivating solutions to work toward and scary because the organization may be averse to change in general, and facing significant uncertainty.

This is the time when the organization starts to lay out a strategic vision for its future and to highlight how the new areas will meet current and projected needs. This process should be complemented by a detailed plan for operationalizing the turnaround over the coming months. (This plan should not be mistaken for the strategic plan that will guide the organization's growth, which will be put together once the organization leaves turnaround.) Outlining the vision and creating a plan are important, not only because they will guide the turnaround but because they help strengthen the organization's planning muscles, ones that it has probably not used much in the past and that will be important moving forward.

Case Study: Through its analysis of the community and through researching alternative service models, MSS determined that there were a couple of directions that it could take. The organization believed that establishing a drop-in center and reconfiguring a section of the organization's current facility to accommodate pregnant women would meet the needs of a growing section of the area's homeless population. These new components were attractive to new private foundations and to several potential major donors in the region, both because of the work MSS had done in building its case and because these components addressed areas of previously unmet need. The drop-in center and the facility for pregnant women diversified both MSS's service offerings and its revenue streams. MSS had been weak in these program areas, and the assessment conducted earlier had shown that funders were looking for an organization that had a multifocus approach to homeless issues and diversified revenue streams.

Collaborating As the organization begins to move forward on a turnaround plan, with clear goals and objectives, it becomes very important that the nonprofit also strengthen its ability to collaborate. Nonprofit organizations are continually flooded with multiple messages about the need and value of collaboration. Funders emphasize it. Conferences are filled with sessions on its value. Yet nonprofit organizations continue to have difficulty using collaboration to help themselves move forward. Organizing meetings and sharing program participants are one part of collaboration, but only scratch the surface of what true collaboration can achieve. For organizations working through the turnaround phase, the ability to collaborate is essential.

A first step would be to ask your organization and potential collaborators a series of questions:

What partnerships exist that will help the organization make a more meaningful impact in the community?

Where can collaboration happen that will help the organization obtain needed resources?

How can other organizations and the community benefit from the new direction of the organization?

How can you bring other organizations and sectors together through your work?

All these questions point to a new path of creating partnerships and connections that can help propel the organization during turnaround. If the answers to these questions align with where you see your organization going, then the next step would be to discuss areas in which the organization can partner.

Case Study: As MSS gained momentum on the new programming and services, including the addition of new donors and private funders, the nonprofit became of interest to other organizations within the community. Some of these only knew MSS as one that had been struggling; for others, the organization's reemergence reminded them of times long ago when MSS had been thriving. Many were somewhere in between. In all cases, the organizations had a new view of MSS in turnaround, and a number of them wanted to be engaged with the effort.

MSS was able to form a collaboration to pursue a federal funding stream aimed at helping low-income people become self-sufficient. New partnerships with the corporate community and with local businesses brought the issue of poverty to new sections of the community. These were some of what became a wildfire of new partnerships that were created to help advance MSS's new direction. Enhancing its ability to collaborate helped MSS when it needed to develop future governmental and private relationships in order to fund new facilities.

Applying Discipline   As the organization moves through the turnaround phase, it begins to abandon the bad practices that led to its decline and adopt new practices that will sustain it once it completes the turnaround. To truly complete a turnaround, the organization must live and breathe its new identity.

If it exhibits old behaviors that could be damaging, it should not move forward until it overcomes them. For example, if an organization has moved through the turnaround phase and still has many of the same board members in many of the same roles, it may not have changed this essential area of the organization. The organization has really only shuffled some pieces around or changed its appearance on the outside, but inside it is still rotting. Applying the new discipline is an important step as the nonprofit emerges from the turnaround phase. Some other critical areas that are likely to need to be changed are programs, systems and infrastructure, and approaches to marketing, communications, and fundraising. If you look at these areas and see many of the old practices, you may be the same emperor but just wearing some new clothes.

Growth Readiness

What phase does an organization move to once it leaves the turnaround phase? The answer to this relates to how much of a DNA change the organization makes. If your organization is one of the few to make a monumental shift in direction, then its new mission idea is very different, and the turnaround would lead into a start-up phase. If the organization is changing much of its skeleton but in terms of mission has made only some shifts in its approach, then the organization may be turning around into a growth phase, essentially building on a restructured program mix that better suits the community and the organization. If you review the start-up and growth chapters of this book, you will see the characteristics that make up those stages and will easily be able to determine where the organization will be restarting on the lifecycle. Whatever phase the nonprofit will be in, it is absolutely essential that its DNA change is complete before restart. A failure to complete the change will leave the organization unprepared to deal with the challenges of growth, and it will likely find itself moving rapidly through the lifecycle toward decline in a very short time frame. As the transformed organization is ready to emerge, adhering to the advice outlined earlier in the book will help it navigate the growth successfully. In addition, having some growth in the organization's history may serve as an additional guiding force in successful growth.

Case Study: After we had moved on from MSS, the organization continued to experience interest from various areas of the community, and it was moving toward a growth position on the lifecycle. It appeared publicly that this was a new organization on the rise, but in practice, MSS had not changed key aspects as it started to grow. Board members were still practicing bad behaviors, such as being involved in day-to-day management and not accepting a fundraising role. Internally, this led to feelings that MSS had not really changed its core, and organizational leaders had a difficult relationship with the board. The nonprofit experienced great program and fundraising success, but there was a lot of turnover among executive directors (EDs) due to the challenges of dealing with the board's management style. Ultimately the board found a leader who was able to work in this environment and has stayed on for several years.

CLOSING AN ORGANIZATION

Perhaps one of the clearest signs that the nonprofit sector had been significantly affected by the 2008 economic crisis was that on any given day in 2010, a Google news search on "nonprofit closing" would yield a dozen or more articles on the closings of nonprofits throughout the United States. On one particular day, the following articles were representative:

- The Surflight Theatre, a New Jersey theater, was facing "deep financial trouble" and could close its doors unless it came up with $500,000 in thirty days, according to the *Atlantic City Press*. Gene Hammond, president of the board of trustees, said that the theater's financial problems have been wearing on officials, stating, "We're constantly in debt, and no matter how we put in plans to reduce the debt, we were spending more money than we were bringing in."[3]

- Group Homes for Children, an Alabama-based nonprofit that had been helping troubled young people since 1973, closed its doors because it could no longer afford to keep them open. "It is not a sustainable operation," Group Homes board chairman Matthew Duke stated in a local Montgomery publication. "It was the most heart-wrenching decision by our board of directors. To see the loss of those services providing our community is heart-wrenching."[4]

- LifeSpan Farm, a therapeutic riding center in North Carolina, closed its doors after nearly forty years of operation. LifeSpan officials say the center lost money annually and they could no longer afford to keep it open, having closed five of its twenty-four programs because of $7 million in government cutbacks over the past two years and a decline in charitable giving, as reported by the *Charlotte Observer*.[5]

In late 2008, Paul Light, an expert in the nonprofit sector and professor at New York University's Wagner School of Public Service, predicted that at least one hundred thousand nonprofits nationwide will be forced to close their doors as a result of the 2008 financial crisis.[6] Although it is not yet clear whether Light's prediction will be borne out, there is no question that many nonprofits are being faced with the decision to close their doors, and the examples here hint at the likelihood that those organizations that were in challenging circumstances before the economic meltdown might find that these challenges expedite their issues and force a closure far faster than they could have imagined.

Looking at Light's prediction, it also is interesting to examine the state of the nonprofit sector to gain a sense of how many organizations really might find themselves in this phase of the nonprofit lifecycle. According to Ron Mattock's book *Zone of Insolvency* and the *Nonprofit Almanac 2008,* by the Urban Institute, there are approximately 1.5 million nonprofit organizations, employing over twelve million employees (10 percent of the U.S. workforce). There are more than twenty million board members, and twenty thousand board meetings are convened each day. Although the sector grows, on average, 3 to 6 percent per year and accounts for approximately 6 percent of the nation's income, an estimated 7 percent of all nonprofits are insolvent, unable to meet their financial obligations.[7] The Nonprofit Finance Fund reported in 2010 that nearly a third of nonprofits did not have enough cash on hand to cover more than one month of expenses and that less than a fifth of nonprofits anticipated being able to cover their operating expenses in 2009 and 2010.[8] Finally, in this vein, the National Education Association reported that joblessness will cost states over $700 billion in revenue, which will enhance the current negative practices of withholding payments to nonprofit organizations and decreasing government support.[9] The conclusion we might draw from these statistics is that although there is growth in the number of nonprofits, a large number of volunteers invested in governing, and a more prominent role for nonprofits in our nation's economy, Light's prediction may be too kind on the sector. Unfortunately, we may see a number that is at least 10 percent higher than his.

THE MIND-SET OF CLOSING ORGANIZATIONS

Oftentimes when you work with organizations that have the word "closing" in their vocabulary, the language used can conjure up metaphors related to death and hospitals. You might hear such words or phrases as "life support" or "fading fast." Staff and leaders experience feelings quite similar to those one might feel when a person is nearing death. In her book *On Death and Dying*, Elisabeth Kübler-Ross outlined the five stages of grief. (Originally the stages were meant to apply to the dying individual, but over time their application was expanded to include survivors, in what is now commonly referred to as the Kübler-Ross model.) These stages are similar to what many organizations experience when the thought of closing their doors becomes very real. The next sections outline the model and how these stages relate to the characteristics and actions exhibited by nonprofit organizations. For each of these areas, we highlight the challenges faced by organizations that fail to move beyond each stage.

Denial

Organizations confronted with the possibility of closing may try to give the impression that all is well and that closing is an overreaction. For an individual, denial is usually only a temporary short-term defense. This is not always the case in an organization, where the decision makers, including senior staff and board members, can often take a great deal of time to come to a consensus on closing. An inability to rally the key stakeholders and obtain consensus jeopardizes the chances of achieving a smooth organizational closing. For an individual, the goal of working through the denial stage is to obtain a heightened awareness of the impact of a life ending. The analogy to the nonprofit is the need to assess the impact of closing on stakeholders, particularly staff and clients or customers. Part of this effort will be to assign clear roles for those participating in the closing of the organization.

An ungraceful closing (one in which the organization closes immediately and without strategy) can occur when leaders fail to agree that the organization does in fact need to close. Several may believe that the organization can still be turned around, even in the face of data that significantly show otherwise. Others, specifically board members, may quickly retreat from the organization, realizing that the job isn't enjoyable for them or that they don't have the energy to confront such challenging circumstances. Worse, they may view the organization as a "sinking ship."

Anger

Once the organization is able to get past denying that closing is a necessity, many individuals or segments of the organization may become angry at having only the single option. An individual facing death might say, "It's not fair!" or "How can this happen to me?" In organizations, the common question often becomes "Who is to blame?" Individuals within the organization may make it very difficult to complete the final work needed to ensure a graceful closing. For some, closing the nonprofit may bring a sense of embarrassment within the broader community or represent an admission that they cannot "fix" the challenged nonprofit, giving them a sense of failure at the inability to change the organization's path.

The organization can develop mechanisms that allow people to work through their anger quickly and possibly to turn the anger into positive energy for the community. The first step would create open spaces, in meetings or separate gatherings, where people have a chance to talk about their perspectives and potentially offer solutions for helping the organization move forward through the closing process.

An ungraceful closing can occur if the anger dominates. As mentioned, an impulse to start blaming individuals for the causes of closing may arise, creating further resentment and strife. Those that close ungracefully often cannot get past this anger. Although these feelings are hard to overcome, the most important part of the organization's legacy will be in how it closes.

Bargaining

The third stage when an individual is dealing with death is to summon an internal hope that he or she can somehow postpone or delay death. People in this stage commonly say things like "If I could just have more time." Organizations engage in similar behavior, often by trying to reach one far-off benchmark. Sometimes this is a last attempt to "save" the nonprofit, but it might also be an attempt to postpone closing. For example, the nonprofit might want to survive long enough to complete its summer programming before closing its doors. Although in some cases such bargaining may fit within the organizational plan to close, in many others it is a significant deviation from the plan that could impair its implementation.

An ungraceful closing can occur when an organization strays significantly from the closure plan. One of us (John) worked with a large national health-related organization that was not able to meet the benchmarks set to fulfill a turnaround. The benchmarks to be reached were a certain level of funding obtained by key donors and the ability to reconfigure current institutional funding so as to give the organization more flexibility to deal with its cash flow challenges. After the closure plan was created, several board members wanted to schedule final closure to occur after a traditional, high-profile public event. The event would occur well after the organization had run through its remaining cash, but the board was determined to produce this event one final time because they had invested so much of their personal time over the years in this event that they almost had more at stake in its production than in the mission of the organization. In addition, some of the board members who advocated for the event still held out a sliver of hope that the event would yield the necessary funding resources to give the nonprofit further life. Unfortunately, financial support from previous event donors and several board members failed to materialize. The organization had to close its doors immediately, with staff members and external partners learning just days before of the organization's unfortunate path. The organization had to close sooner than it had planned because the board had bargained into holding an event that ultimately hurt its ability to reach its organizational benchmarks. Rethinking the event might have been a more effective strategy in the long run.

Depression

Depression is the most commonly identified feeling experienced by those facing a death or a closure. An individual suffering after a death may become silent, refuse visitors, and spend much of the time crying and grieving. They may disconnect from love and affection. Although the feelings experienced during an organizational closure are not identical to those of losing a loved one to death, there are important similarities. In the depression phase, organizations recognize that the organization is going to close and will cease to exist. This can cause stakeholders to withdraw, believing that closing out the organization is too difficult.

Although the closure may be on a fast track due to a variety of factors, it is also important for organizational leaders to offer pathways for people to grieve. The challenge becomes organizing the balance between allowing people to express their sadness while also implementing the closure plan. Spending too much time focused on processing feelings of depression will jeopardize the closure plan; but if you rush into the closure plan without creating avenues for people to communicate their sense of loss, you run the risk of making closure even more difficult.

Acceptance

In the final stage, the organization has worked through its grief, and the remaining staff and volunteers have committed to the plan and are working toward a positive closure. Through the previous four stages, there will have been a natural peel of former supporters, and those remaining are usually a much smaller group. One of the important responsibilities for leadership at this time is to consistently highlight the successes of the organization, talking about the positive impacts it has made, the relationships it has forged, and the lasting legacy it will leave behind. This focus on the upside can be a driving force behind leaving a valuable legacy for an organization and creating a more positive experience for those departing, who still feel a close connection to the nonprofit. The most damaging thing an organization can do at this stage is to be too focused on the closing plan and fail to highlight the great aspects of the nonprofit and its history.

TURNAROUND INTERVIEW

A nationally recognized nonprofit leader and consultant, Jan Glick has devoted more than twenty-five years to refining a model approach to facilitate performance improvement for nonprofits and government agencies. Glick is the author of *Nonprofit Turnaround: A Guide for Nonprofit Leaders, Consultants and Funders.*

As you think about organizations in the turnaround phase, what are the characteristics of an organization that successfully navigates turnaround, and what are the characteristics of groups that have trouble moving through turnaround?

Imagine that every organization has four gas tanks that measure human capacity, financial capacity, and, while they may not be capacities in the conventional sense, a tank measuring the power of the organization's mission and programs, and a final one that measures the capacity of its internal systems.

Organizations that have a critical mass of "gas," or capacity, in these four tanks can successfully weather the challenges of crisis and turnaround. Those whose capacities in these four areas fall short will either fail or at best limp along barely surviving.

Now the human capacity is by far the most important, because people can generate money, build internal systems, and adjust and improve the organization's programs. So the most critical characteristic of an organization that successfully navigates a turnaround is the strength, commitment, caliber, and ability of its people to work together, to fix the organization's problems, and lead it toward programmatic and financial success. However, it is important to remember that this capacity is the most common problem that organizations in crisis have—that people, culture, and communications problems are prevalent in all of the 111 turnaround cases studied for *Nonprofit Turnaround.* Therein lies the paradox: it takes people power to solve the problems that were, in largest part, caused by the individuals involved in the first place. Which of course serves as a reminder of the prevalence of board and staff turnover to successfully execute a turnaround. To this end, the leaders' ability to move beyond their previous cultural and communications problems and harness their collective energies and ideas can sometimes be stimulated or led by a new turnaround leader.

Regardless of how precisely full the human gas tank is, having sufficient capacity in the other tanks might be enough to stave off closure and succeed in a turnaround, as long as there is a reasonable amount of human motivation, skill, and commitment left. But if the cultural and communications dysfunction is severe enough, staff, board, and other volunteers can easily burn out (if they aren't already burned out prior to identifying the crisis in the first place) attempting to raise money, fix the business model or internal systems, and so on.

But to consider the other three gas tanks further, let's assume for a moment that in a given organization facing a crisis, the human capacity is sufficient that the organization won't fall apart for that reason alone. Let's assume that this organization declined because of changing market conditions that depleted revenues, taxed internal systems, and made the mission and business model at least partially obsolete. And for this analysis, we can assume that people and communication problems exist, but they are modest.

In this case, the factors which would determine whether the organization can survive and succeed in the turnaround effort are represented by the collective gas left in all four tanks. If the relevance of the mission is sufficiently obsolete, for example, it will be extraordinarily difficult for the organization to raise enough money to support its programs the way it used to. Such an organization then either has to be very good at rebranding itself and/or modify mission and program mix to meet new market conditions. In the latter case, the business model, internal systems, and quite possibly some of the board and staff may also have to change to align with the new program direction. Too much change of this sort is difficult and therefore expensive enough (in people's time and energy as well as financial cost) to doom even well-thought-out turnaround plans. People burn out and can't stick it out long enough to succeed, and/or money runs out.

Experienced turnaround leaders can often gauge, or have a personal feeling, of whether any particular turnaround process is likely to succeed or is more likely to fail based on the amount of gas their assessment indicates is left in these four tanks. Such leaders will tend to have enough information to have an opinion either at the conclusion of their assessment process or relatively soon afterwards. Which leads to the final characteristic that a successful turnaround candidate must have: some self-assessment capability.

Even if the turnaround leader has a strong feeling about the chances of success based on their assessment findings and experience in similar situations, the more collective self-assessment capacity the board and management team have is certainly a significant factor that plays into an organization's chances for success.

What is important to know and understand about turnaround when a group is starting a decline? Are there things they should think about long before a potential turnaround can happen?

The earlier an organization takes notice of a decline, the greater its chances are of stemming the tide and turning it around. Early in a decline, an organization is not faced with the severity of time and financial pressure that exists when human and financial assets run down further. If the organization has not applied several basic management practices in the past, it still has time to take notice of its deteriorating position and begin to take action. And well-managed, well-governed organizations don't ever allow a decline to go very far, because they implement five assessment practices regularly, and have the experience and skill to act on the findings to limit any decline to modest proportions. Such organizations implement regular assessments of the following five key elements of organizational capacity factors approximately annually:

1. *Executive director performance.* Comprehensive annual evaluation by the board with input from staff and external stakeholders.

2. *Board of directors performance.* Annual, objective self-evaluation, including an honest assessment of whether the organization has a board and decision-making processes that are capable of making the tough decisions as indicated by organizational and market assessment, and making them expeditiously.

3. *Market analysis.* Objectively answering the key questions: Does the need for the organization and its programs remain high enough to justify existing programs, or are changes called for? Similarly, are funders still interested in supporting the organization's programs? What other external, operating environment changes may affect the organization and its programs?

4. *Financial position and effectiveness of business model.* This assessment goes far beyond an audit, which describes an organization's financial position and financial controls. Evaluation of the business model answers questions such as whether the revenue mix is optimal, what expense categories may be excessive, how each program area is performing on its own, are internal systems efficient, and are programs aligned with market demand. In addition, regular assessment of whether financial reports for the board and the management team are adequate to describe the business model and the organization's relative efficiency and effectiveness at executing its model are critical for openness and transparency, to allow all

key leaders to base their input and dialogue on relevant and complete data.

5. *Staff performance evaluations.* Similar to the executive director evaluation, this is a comprehensive annual evaluation by the supervisor, ideally with input from other key staff and stakeholders with whom the individual works regularly.

While there is no existing research data that informs us as to what percentage of our sector employs all these management techniques annually, I estimate that these are performed collectively in less than 10 percent of nonprofits, and that these organizations are the largest nonprofits in the sector. Anecdotal comments from many nonprofit leaders over the years indicate that each individual assessment in the list is performed in less than half of nonprofits on an annual basis. However, these oversight functions are truly fundamental fiduciary responsibilities. Responsibility for their implementation should be appropriately shared between a governing board and management team, which, if competent, will at least take a stab at performing these analyses to some degree each year. And if such an organization can both (1) gather such data and (2) act on it, objectively, its chances of slipping into a long decline leading to crisis are small.

As you think about the nonprofit sector today, with the current economy, the pending leadership gap, and the current funding environment, what are areas of innovation that nonprofits can think of in light of these challenges?

I believe that on the whole, what nonprofits need the most is not innovation but the courage and skill to take action on business fundamentals. Accurately assessing an organization's internal and market situation, taking action on the findings, and having the courage to make what are often difficult decisions regarding cutting back or changing programs and real people—all these things remain elusive for many nonprofits. What may be easy decisions for a corporation—divesting a line of business, terminating staff, even asking a board member to step down—often remain difficult, hand-wringing decisions for many nonprofit staff and board members to implement. This discomfort with tough decisions is, in large part, due to the fact that many nonprofit board leaders are typically involved because of a passion for the organization's services, and don't necessarily bring business skills or business thinking to the table. Similarly, nonprofit staff leaders often rise up through the ranks with a background in the organization's functional specialty, without ever getting much management or leadership training.

Even what the nonprofit sector considers innovation represents fairly common management practice in the corporate world. For example, here are a few practices that I've observed nonprofits take recently, listed in order of increasing innovation, as defined by how frequently similar practices are applied in the corporate world. These practices offer great benefit to nonprofits and would benefit others greatly by broader application. Each successive practice in the list builds on the implications of the earlier points.

Shared or outsourced administrative services. Several nonprofits from noncompeting subsectors can partner with each other to share back-end services, such as database administration, HR services, technology support, and other administrative functions. Such work, duplicated by thousands of small nonprofits, simply drives up overhead costs, sapping donors' funds and, worse yet, because of the very fact that most nonprofits are tiny, often is performed highly inefficiently. Such back-end systems are often outsourced in the private sector, allowing corporations to focus sharply on their core missions, build and apply their core competencies, and avoid overspending on inefficient internal systems. Yet nonprofits typically shy away from this sort of deep partnership for two reasons. First, there is an extensive up-front investment in time and energy, and ongoing coordination is required for such shared services to work well. But perhaps the larger perceived barrier is the disclosure of records and competition for donors that this example resolves by forming a partnership among agencies from different subsectors. While an environmental organization may well share donors with a human services agency, the frequency that this occurs is greatly reduced, and therefore the chances for such a partnership to succeed are much better.

Partnerships, mergers, consolidation. The number of nonprofits in the United States continues to climb each year, outpacing the increase in charitable giving even prior to the start of the recession that began in 2007. Our sector's continued addition of thousands of small nonprofits breeds duplication and a dilution of the impact of donor dollars across thousands of small organizations that research shows haven't got the capacity to manage [themselves] effectively. Moving beyond the administrative partnership example above, program partnerships up to and including mergers offer a real possibility for achieving greater capacity and effectiveness.

Funder incentives for capacity building and funder collaboration. While funders and nonprofit leaders have for many years discussed the pressing need for efficiencies to be gained through partnerships, mergers, and consolidations, only a tiny percentage of funders actually support such efforts with real dollars. Yet funders occupy a catbird's seat when it comes to innovation. Any good nonprofit leader has learned to navigate the foundation grant-making arena and tailor grant proposals to funder interest areas. Yet very few foundations support capacity building, which, according to data from Philanthropy Northwest, accounts for approximately 1 percent of institutional giving from its membership of over one thousand foundations. However, each of the practices in this list requires a significant front-end investment that in many cases represents a huge stretch for an individual organization's capacity to launch. The survival and thriving of the sector demands that funders also need to change their approach to funding to foster innovation on organizational practices and not limit such incentives to program innovation. Were funders willing to increase their capacity building investment, and target it toward the sort of innovative practices noted here, their support could truly catalyze innovation applied systematically to a growing number of nonprofits.

For example, funders can, and a few have, provided a safe "open space" for nonprofits within the same arena to discuss partnership and merger possibilities without feeling forced, and support such discussions with real dollars. Increases in such pilot approaches would likely lead to a resulting increase in partnership and merger activity, and thereby greater efficiency and capacity developed. However, funders themselves need to be innovative beyond simply adding capacity building to their giving guidelines. As with any other program, the cost for a nonprofit to be able to successfully analyze a merger's feasibility and then execute it likely requires funding from more than one source, meaning that funders need to explicitly and formally collaborate—something that is as uncommon in the grant-making world as it is among grantees.

Leveraging volunteers' time and skills across more functions. Based on the work of the Taproot Foundation and others, nonprofits that invest in planning for and fully leveraging the use of volunteers far beyond rote tasks—indeed in key traditional staff roles as well, such as management, marketing, IT, and human resources—demonstrate strong returns on such investments. When coupled with the need for more effective boards and today's bleak economic landscape, investment in volunteerism is an especially relevant innovation strategy.

TURNAROUND—PROJECT REACH YOUTH CASE STUDY

Much of the work that John does is dedicated to working with organizations in crisis, often engaging in turnaround efforts. In this case study, John discusses his work with Project Reach Youth, an effort that he ultimately led through a successful merger.

PRY's Founding

Project Reach Youth was founded in 1968 as a small program of a church in Park Slope, Brooklyn. Phil West, one of the founders, discussed the founding of PRY in a blog post on PRY's fortieth anniversary:

> PRY began at the Park Slope United Methodist Church in 1968, a turbulent year in our neighborhood and our nation. The Vietnam

War wrenched our national consciousness. Many turned against Dr. Martin Luther King, Jr., when he began to preach against the war. The Slope seethed with ethnic tensions. Booze, grass, and glue, not to mention harder drugs, were everywhere. Young teens were getting stoned.

What could a neighborhood church without money do but open its doors?

Monte Clinton, who became Lay Leader in 1968, coined the name PRY (Project Reach Youth). I remember him explaining the acronym at the congregation's annual meeting. "PRY," he said, "has two purposes. The first is to pry young people off the street corner outside and get them into our church basement for programs that will help them survive and thrive. The second is to pry members of our congregation out of these pews and get us helping as teachers and mentors."

Pastor Klaus Kingsdorf from St. John-St. Matthew-Emanuel Lutheran Church on 7th Street embraced that vision, and he made contact with Wagner College, which has deep roots in the Lutheran tradition. We opened the doors for Friday night programs, and kids came. But before long, Monte and other leaders spent every Friday afternoon chasing around for tools, wood, fabric, paint, glue, flour, cookies, fruit juice. Every week, a caravan of cars headed out to Staten Island for the Wagner students who became mentors. More important than the projects were relationships and conversations. Lots of voices until 9:00, and then students walking kids home. After clean-up and debriefing, back into cars for the trip back across the new Verrazano-Narrows Bridge.

Within a year, we saw how many youth needed homework help, and we added tutoring programs on Tuesday nights. College trips came later.

Growth and Expansion

Project Reach Youth, Inc., became one of Brooklyn's most respected community-based organizations committed to helping low-income youths, adults, and families to learn and grow in a creative and supportive environment. Growing from 1968, PRY provided thousands of participants with opportunities to reach their goals and embark on paths to brighter futures through education, training, and counseling.

In 2007, PRY offered a comprehensive array of educational services to the families of Brooklyn, many of whom face the difficulties of poverty, high unemployment, limited English proficiency, and low educational attainment. PRY's programming is intergenerational, and educational services are offered for all ages beginning at infancy. All PRY programs support community members in developing a variety of skills that will help them succeed personally, academically, and professionally, and each component is part of a deliberately holistic approach to education and youth development. As a result of PRY's long and substantial relationship with the communities it serves, the organization and its staff are in a unique position to provide a strategic and innovative curriculum that meets the needs of the people it serves.

PRY's programs addressed the academic and social-emotional needs of low-income families in Brooklyn. The neighborhoods PRY served included the South Park Slope, Sunset Park, Fort Green, Bushwick, and Borough Park communities, all of which had low educational attainment and income levels. These neighborhoods face a number of challenges, including New York City's lowest literacy rates and highest unemployment rates, a disproportionate incidence of HIV/AIDS, and high rates of drug and alcohol addiction.

PRY's best years occurred in the late 1980s to late 1990s, when a strong ED expanded programming and diversified its funding with local government and foundations. John Nuzum, a PRY board member for nearly two decades and eventual board treasurer, stated that "The ED was a great fundraiser, had great support internally and great confidence from the funders, especially family funders." In the late 1990s, a difficult leadership transition with the same strong but founderlike ED followed, accompanied by high staff turnover, a deteriorating financial condition, and the belief that program quality was dropping. In addition, during the organization's growth and through the decline, PRY's infrastructure did not grow with the organization.

In 2007, after over seven years of either challenged or interim leadership, the organization was looking to turn itself around. According to Nuzum, "PRY limped along for about eight years without any working capital. The successor ED lost confidence of the funders and did not have the ability to network and maintain contacts as the previous ED." As Nuzum thought about the point that started PRY's demise, he cited that "the ED left to start a new organization and when she left to that effort, so did many of the funders. The board did not have an active role in fundraising." Nuzum and the rest of the board were not able to forecast that this spin-off would have a growing negative impact on the organization for the next several years, and when the new ED was unable to maintain the same fundraising prowess, the board was unprepared. "The departing ED had a business plan for the spin-off, but PRY did not have a business plan" when the ED left.

Challenge

In 2007, PRY hired a new executive director (author John Brothers) to lead the organization through tough times. The previous ED and PRY had parted ways more than a year before, and the organization had been run by the deputy director since that time. Immediately upon hire, John began a thorough organizational analysis and strategic discussion to get a clear picture of the external and internal landscape. Several consultants were brought on board to look specifically at various areas within the organization. One of the reports stated that the hire of the new ED afforded PRY a real opportunity by bringing new energy and a heightened sense of accountability for board and staff leadership. PRY also had been hampered by difficulties for several years, including a declining reputation with funders, questions about program quality, a severely weakened financial condition, and a board that was not seen as accountable or actively engaged. As the challenges became more difficult, the board was forced to take a more active role. Nuzum stated, "The board was now performing in roles that it had not before and now had an active management role" in the organization.

In order for the organizational turnaround to succeed, the organization would have to focus on several important areas, including delivering quality programs that were guided by program measurement, strong fundraising, board responsibility, and financial soundness/transparency. Discussing their concern about PRY during interviews conducted in 2007, funders stated: "I am a strong advocate for PRY here at the Foundation. But it is getting harder to convince my colleagues to stay the course. We've been worried about PRY" and "PRY used to be a high priority for us. Now they have to be a low priority until the problems are fixed." As PRY began to tackle the identified issues, the fundraising effort became more and more central. Financial analysis highlighted major challenges with regard to the cash flow available to the organization. A portion of PRY's CCAT assessment is included in the Appendix; it provides a sense of the organizational deficiencies.

Next Steps and Final Outcome

Once the ED finished his organizational and community assessment, the organization began a series of program and infrastructure upgrades, including some program and staff reductions. The goal for the organization after the assessment and the meeting with funders was to reduce some immediate costs, shrink the challenges to cash flow, concentrate specifically on programs that PRY could do well, and address some low-hanging organizational issues like a new Web site and upgraded communications materials. These efforts would reduce costs, enhance services, and move some of the dissatisfied funders back into a funding relationship.

Despite all of this change, however, the organization was still very much a "cash-flow" organization, meaning that the cash situation had become so serious that the organization's ability to meet day-to-day cash needs (payroll, line of credit, vendors, and so on) dominated its short-term strategy. The board and ED worked out a scenario plan that outlined dates and specific actions that would be taken on those dates depending on cash flow position and fundraising expectations. Actions linked to these benchmark dates included cutting additional programming, beginning discussions with potential merger candidates, engaging with state government officials on transferring programs away from PRY, and closing PRY's doors.

As the first benchmark date passed without the organization's meeting the revenue goals it had established for itself in deciding to continue on as an organization, PRY created a list of five potential merger candidates that met the predetermined merger criteria that were important to PRY. One of the positive aspects of spending several months solidifying infrastructure was that in many organizational areas there were infrastructure upgrades that made the organization more attractive to potential merger candidates.

Once the merger list was narrowed down to two candidates, PRY began a due diligence process with each candidate that included interviews and the reviewing of finances and programs. Immediately following the PRY board meeting with each organization's leadership, PRY chose to form a strategic alliance with Lutheran Family Health Centers, a long-serving hospital system that included extensive community programming. "For four decades, our two efforts have provided similar and complementary services in South Brooklyn. By joining forces, we will create a stronger organization and provide a more secure safety net to the underserved," said Bob Schwed, PRY's board president. "We both have a great deal to offer the other." Larry McReynolds, ED of Lutheran Family Health Centers, stated, "We are excited about continuing and enhancing the valuable programs of Project Reach Youth. It's beneficial for all involved, especially the community and those we serve." As the merge began to finalize, many of the staff, clients, and partners remained intact and now were intertwined with a larger cadre of other programs and services, which ultimately served the community more effectively.

A couple years after the merger, Schwed observed that it had "good synergy" and that the organizations were "compatible. Programs are running well and by and large things are moving." As Schwed thought about the final years, he saw some good in the crisis: "We had a great team" as PRY headed into the merge. One former board member recently sent an e-mail to those who were there at the end, stating "PRY lives on!" PRY's merger partner, Lutheran, won a huge federal grant funding many of the areas that PRY used to and continues to serve. PRY, now part of another organization but still retaining many of the staff who had been brought over, continues working on the great initiatives that marked its high point in the late 1990s.

chapter SEVEN

Conclusion

According to the Aspen Institute, America's nonprofit sector currently confronts a variety of challenges that it only dimly understands and for which it is not well prepared, including the following:

- Demographic shifts that are expanding the "market" for the services that nonprofits provide
- Commercial pressures that are pushing nonprofits into greater reliance on fee-for-service income
- Expanded competition from for-profit providers
- Opposition to nonprofit advocacy activity
- Challenges to nonprofit tax-exempt status
- Increased accountability pressures
- Rapidly changing communications technology

Aspen's findings correlate with those of the national research conducted by Guidestar focused on what nonprofits feel are their biggest challenges and obstacles to success, which respondents viewed as (1) obtaining resources, (2) having successful boards, and (3) being able to communicate effectively. The demand for nonprofits to document the quality and impact of their work is only increasing, exacerbated by other, sometimes contradictory factors, such as a growing leadership shortage and a new economic reality for the sector. In short, the imperative of "effectiveness" is only becoming more urgent in the nonprofit sector.

In the face of these challenges, getting an organization to a better place is fundamentally about embracing the concept of change. A whole host of tools and processes exist to help nonprofit leaders take on such initiatives: business planning, strategic planning, evaluation, coaching, retreats, and more. Yet although we have learned a lot about the mechanics of these processes, too often the results (the plan, the financial model, the board structure, and so on) are not successfully implemented. This begs at least two questions: (1) Why? and (2) How can we turn this around? Change is inevitable, important, and really difficult. Nonprofit leaders need to facilitate it in a more thoughtful, structured, and deliberate way, but one size does not fit all; the challenges and solutions are likely to look different depending on where an organization is in its lifecycle.

With these perspectives and in the face of the current economic crisis, this book focused on fulfilling a sectorwide need for tools that allow practitioners to understand where they are in respect to other nonprofit organizations; they also must have access to resources, best practices, and case studies to draw on for guidance on how they should proceed. We directed this book to look at the wide-ranging analysis of hundreds of nonprofit organizations throughout the United States in various areas of organizational effectiveness. We hope that practitioners and nonprofit leaders, as well as the academic community dedicated to the nonprofit sector, will find great value in this research and its practical application.

REFLECTIONS ON THIS BOOK

As we were writing this book, we had a number of conversations about what growth can and should mean as a driving force in nonprofit development and change. Does growth mean *expansion* in the absolute terms (bigger budgets, more staff, more people reached), or should we talk about it in terms of *improvement*? We recognize, of course, that this is a false dichotomy. Growth should not be an end in and of itself; it is a means to an end—in this case, increased impact and progress toward the achievement of mission. Depending on where an organization is in its lifecycle development, growth might mean bigger numbers, or it might be about doing the job better in some way or another. Or it may be both. Life is like that.

What we tried to do in this book was use complementary lifecycle models as a backdrop for understanding organizational growth and change *as a pathway to increased impact and progress toward achieving mission.* Our intent was to provide you with a way to identify what your organization development priorities might be through identifying your nonprofit's lifecycle phase, and to offer some practical tools to help your organization advance. In recapping the overarching themes in this book, we note the following:

When it comes to growth, more often than not, slow and steady wins the race. The lesson of the high-arc/low-arc model is that a slower, more deliberate approach to growth is probably more sustainable in the long run. Of course, there are times when growth needs to occur quickly. In such cases, we would caution you to be mindful of putting into place, as possible, the systems that will sustain growth. And don't equate rapid growth with effectiveness. Be vigilant for the signs of decline. And know when to stop growing, or at least when to hit the pause button. Let impact be your guide.

Adaptive leadership is the key to sustainable growth. Leaders who understand the importance of collecting information from within and outside the organization and using data to learn and improve are much more likely to have successful organizations.[1] Self-assessment is a theme throughout this book. Regardless of the lifecycle phase an organization is in, a strong assessment is the starting point for better understanding, which can then lead to efforts to improve. We discuss two assessment tools in this book: the Core Capacity Assessment Tool (CCAT) and the Core Support Evaluation (CSE).

Mission, organizational vision, and values are the touchstones that should drive every activity, whether it's the implementation of programs, purchasing of software, or development of a strategic plan. They are the tent under which everything in your organization should fit. From time to time, they should be assessed for clarity and relevance and revised as needed.

The logic model is your friend. When we started writing this book, we intended to discuss the logic model only in the chapter on core program, but found that it kept popping up in other places as well. It is worth the time and effort required to get it right. Like mission, vision, and values, the logic model needs to be revisited to test whether the underlying assumptions related to outcomes and program strategy still hold true.

Founder's syndrome—not just for founders anymore. Founder's syndrome is a challenge that is marked by negative behaviors, not by the presence of the individual who began the nonprofit. Any time the mission, vision, or values of an organization are tightly held by an individual or a small group of leaders, the organization is at risk of decreased effectiveness.

Trust is essential. This is true regardless of lifecycle stage, and is particularly true in times of growth and change, which are often challenging and almost always stressful. If there is a golden rule to be applied, we think it's the first principle from *The Source:* "Exceptional boards govern in constructive partnership with the chief executive, recognizing that the effectiveness of the board and chief executive are interdependent. They build this partnership through trust, candor, respect, and honest communication."[2]

The role of leadership will evolve as the organization does. We cannot over-emphasize our belief that the quality of the board-ED relationship can make or break an organization's ability to become stronger and reach its potential to fulfill mission. It is an important consideration at any phase of the lifecycle.

Be deliberate in understanding the culture of your organization, and then set about articulating the culture you wish to build. Like mission, organizational vision, and values, organizational culture can serve as an important touchstone for making decisions related to growth and organizational improvement.

Reaching the "top" of the lifecycle does not mean your journey has ended. Although the MIE organization may appear to have everything all figured out, it has to work at least as hard as its colleagues that are at other phases of the lifecycle. The challenges for the MIE organization are to expand on its achievements, continue to improve, and maximize impact by sharing its knowledge and expertise with external stakeholders.

Resource development is much more than writing proposals or annual appeals. To a large extent, it is about intertwining strong and authentic relationships with institutional donors, while increasing your organization's profile among external stakeholders. Donors aren't the only ones who have resources you need.

Beware of decline. Most organizations that fall into decline do so without realizing what is happening. Telltale warning signs of decline include fraying in the quality of your programs, complacency on the part of the board of directors, and a community that has shifted while you weren't paying attention. How you react to the situation is as important as the realization, and it is during this time that you will see whether you can turn around.

Turnaround is about taking risks that are big but also well informed. The organization that goes into decline is one whose leaders lack adaptive capacity. Recall that adaptive capacity is about making changes based on good data. An organization that seeks to engage in a turnaround process must embrace change in nearly every area and be willing to accept all the risks a turnaround presents. But remember that these are calculated risks, based on informed decisions and the best data available.

WHERE DO WE GO FROM HERE?

The entire premise of the lifecycle is based on the assumption that *to get where you want to go, you need first to know where you are.* Too often, nonprofits do not first assess the problem before determining the solution. Our hope is that the nonprofit leaders who read this book come away appreciating the importance of an honest and constructive understanding of themselves as a necessary first step in any change effort. We recognize that this can be really hard, but as we noted at the beginning of this book, part of the value of the lifecycle, we think, is that it normalizes the challenges that most nonprofits face. The high-arc/low-arc model is a strong reminder of the importance of rate of growth as an organization seeks to move forward. Our wish is that as you move forward, you are better prepared with a clearer, more objective sense of your organization's strengths and weaknesses and armed with tools to help you successfully manage the challenges you face on the lifecycle journey.

APPENDIX

This appendix includes the following elements:

Table A.1, a Board Report Card template; we discuss the Board Report Card in detail in Chapter Four, and a sample report card is included there (Table 4.2).

Table A.2, the sample cash flow statement cited in Chapter Five; it illustrates a pending cash flow crisis.

Figure A.1, a SPOT analysis template.

Figure A.2, a section of the CCAT report for Project Reach Youth, which we discuss as a case study in Chapter Six.

TABLE A.1

Board Report Card Template

Summary of Activities for: XXXX, member since 00/00/0000

Joined Board: 00/00/0000   Term Ends: 00/00/0000

20XX–XX Committee Recommendation: XXXX Committee   Committee History: XXXX Committee, 0000–0000

XXXX Committee, 0000–0000

Next Role: (e.g., Executive Committee, Leadership Council, Friends of, etc.)

Stated Goals for 20XX: [previous year]

History

	20XX	20XX	20XX
Meeting Attendance:	X of X (XXX%)	X of X (XXX%)	X of X (XXX%)
Committee Attendance:	XXXX Committee	XXXX Committee	XXXX Committee
	X of X meetings	X of X meetings	X of X meetings
Total Board Giving:	$000.00	$000.00	$000.00
Giving:	$000.00	$000.00	$000.00
Getting:	$000.00	$000.00	$000.00

Other Resources: [list]

Event Participation: [list]

Other Participation: (e.g., Participation in strategic planning)

Relevant Background History with _____ :   (e.g., Invited to board by . . .)

Stated Goals for 20XX:

Stated Goals for 20XX:

Stated Goals for 20XX:

TABLE A.2
Sample Cash Flow Statement for a Small Nonprofit

8-June	1 June	8 June	15 June	22 June	29 June	6 July	13 July	20 July	27 July	3 Aug.	11 Aug.	18 Aug.	25 Aug.
Opening Balance (Net)	71,243	69,887	64,951	69,196	60,978	67,241	65,542	57,892	48,168	59,763	58,287	53,237	51,251
Cash Inflows:													
Government	0	0	2,500	0	0	0	0	3,028	0	0	0	0	2,534
Foundation	0	0	0	0	25,000	0	0	0	0	0	0	0	0
Individual/Event	0	64	5,000	0	0	0	0	0	29,750	0	0	0	0
Misc. Income	0	0	0	0	0	0	0	0	0	0	0	0	0
Loan + Other	0	0	0	0	0	0	0	0	0	0	0	0	0
Subtotal Revenue:	0	64	7,500	0	25,000	0	0	3,028	29,750	0	0	0	2,534
Cash Outflows:													
Payroll	1,33ç6	5,000	2,250	0	17,179	1,336	7,250	2,500	17,679	1,336	4,750	1,500	17,679
Fixed	20	0	0	486	0	363	0	486	0	140	0	486	0
Variable	0	0	1,005	7,732	1,558	0	400	9,766	476	0	300	0	476
BNJ + Other	0	0	0	0	0	0	0	0	0	0	0	0	0
Expense Adjustment(s)	0	0	0	0	0	0	0	0	0	0	0	0	0
Subtotal Expense:	1,356	5,000	3,255	8,218	18,737	1,699	7,650	12,752	18,155	1,476	5,050	1,986	18,155
Closing Balance:	69,887	64,951	69,196	60,978	67,241	65,542	57,892	48,168	59,763	58,287	53,237	51,251	35,630
	1 June	8 June	15 June	22 June	29 June	6 July	13 July	20 July	27 July	3 Aug.	11 Aug.	18 Aug.	25 Aug.

Figure A.1
SPOT Analysis

S	Strengths	P	Problems
	• A		• A
	• B		• B
	• C		• C
	• D		• D
	• E		• E
	• F		• F

O	Opportunities	T	Threats
	• A		• A
	• B		• B
	• C		• C
	• D		• D
	• E		• E
	• F		• F

Figure A.2
Section of Project Reach Youth CCAT Report

Core Capacities and Subcapacities	Score*
ADAPTIVE CAPACITY OVERALL	**202**
Organizational Learning	188
Decision-Making Tools	207
Organizational Resource Sustainability	153
Programmatic Learning	180
Environmental Learning	237
Program Resource Adaptability	223
LEADERSHIP CAPACITY OVERALL	**194**
Internal Leadership	215
Leader Vision	249
Leadership Sustainability	153
Board Leadership	164
Leader Influence	217
MANAGEMENT CAPACITY OVERALL	**200**
Assessing Staff Performance	159
Managing Performance Expectations	213
Managing Program Staff	209
Volunteer Management	173
Manager-to-Staff Communication	211
Program Staffing	233
Conveying Unique Value of Staff	192
Problem Solving	220
Staff Development	230
Supporting Staff Resource Needs	154
Financial Management	195
TECHNICAL CAPACITY OVERALL	**180**
Technology Skills	186
Technology	175

Figure A.2
Section of Project Reach Youth CCAT Report (*continued*)

Core Capacities and Subcapacities	Score*
Service Delivery	220
Program Evaluation Skills	200
Outreach	174
Marketing Skills	162
Legal Skills	229
Fundraising Skills	156
Financial Management Skills	192
Facility Management	191
Facilities	108
ORGANIZATIONAL CULTURE OVERALL	208
Unifying	185
Empowering	228
Reenergizing	203

* A score of 230 or higher is a "strength." A score of 191 to 229 is considered "satisfactory." Lower than 191 is a "challenge."

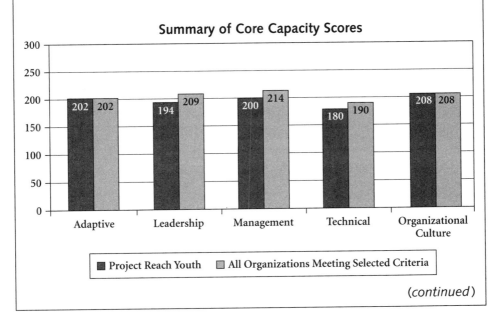

Summary of Core Capacity Scores

Project Reach Youth / All Organizations Meeting Selected Criteria

- Adaptive: 202 / 202
- Leadership: 194 / 209
- Management: 200 / 214
- Technical: 180 / 190
- Organizational Culture: 208 / 208

(*continued*)

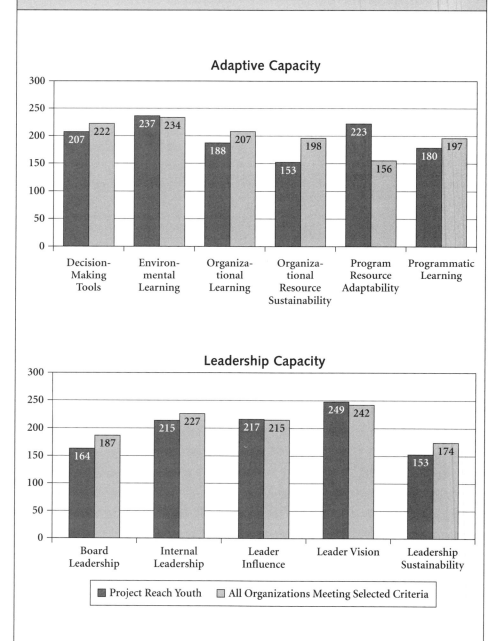

Figure A.2
Section of Project Reach Youth CCAT Report (*continued*)

Adaptive Capacity

Category	Project Reach Youth	All Organizations Meeting Selected Criteria
Decision-Making Tools	207	222
Environmental Learning	237	234
Organizational Learning	188	207
Organizational Resource Sustainability	153	198
Program Resource Adaptability	223	156
Programmatic Learning	180	197

Leadership Capacity

Category	Project Reach Youth	All Organizations Meeting Selected Criteria
Board Leadership	164	187
Internal Leadership	215	227
Leader Influence	217	215
Leader Vision	249	242
Leadership Sustainability	153	174

■ Project Reach Youth   ▨ All Organizations Meeting Selected Criteria

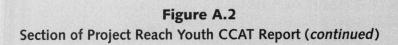

Figure A.2
Section of Project Reach Youth CCAT Report (*continued*)

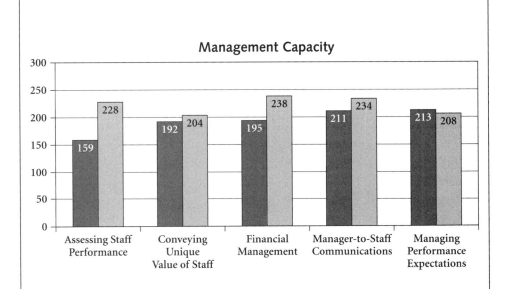

Management Capacity

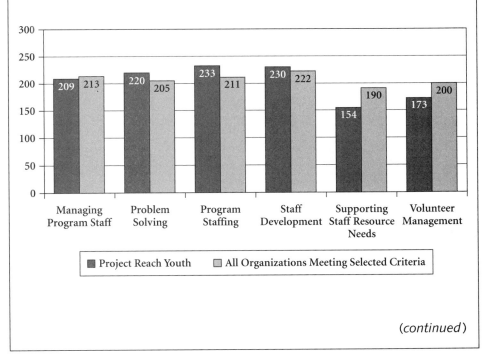

(*continued*)

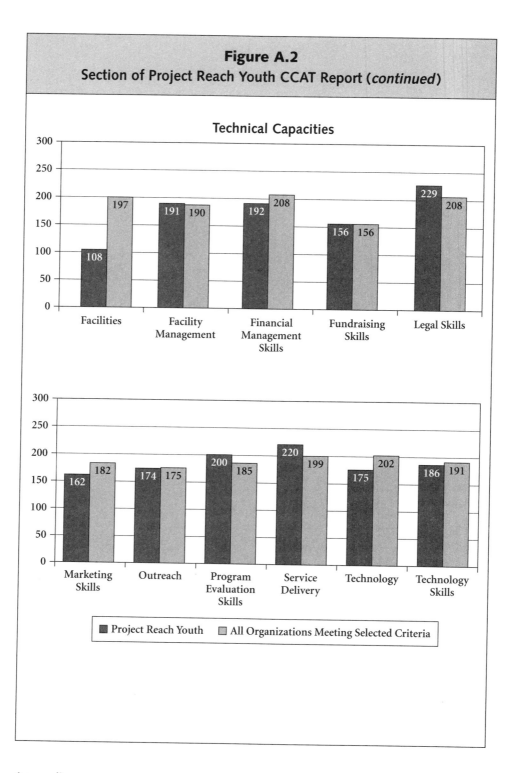

Figure A.2
Section of Project Reach Youth CCAT Report (*continued*)

Technical Capacities

	Project Reach Youth	All Organizations Meeting Selected Criteria
Facilities	108	197
Facility Management	191	190
Financial Management Skills	192	208
Fundraising Skills	156	156
Legal Skills	229	208
Marketing Skills	162	182
Outreach	174	175
Program Evaluation Skills	200	185
Service Delivery	220	199
Technology	175	202
Technology Skills	186	191

■ Project Reach Youth   ☐ All Organizations Meeting Selected Criteria

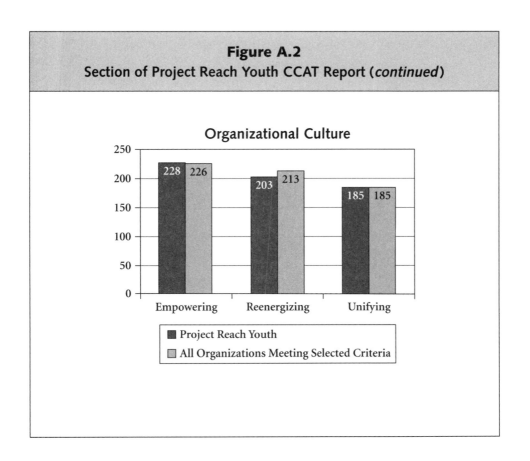

Figure A.2
Section of Project Reach Youth CCAT Report (*continued*)

Organizational Culture

Empowering: Project Reach Youth 228, All Organizations Meeting Selected Criteria 226
Reenergizing: Project Reach Youth 203, All Organizations Meeting Selected Criteria 213
Unifying: Project Reach Youth 185, All Organizations Meeting Selected Criteria 185

■ Project Reach Youth
□ All Organizations Meeting Selected Criteria

NOTES

CHAPTER ONE

1. Susan Kenny Stevens, *Nonprofit Lifecycles: Stage-Based Wisdom for Nonprofit Capacity* (Longlake, MN: Stagewise Enterprises, 2001).

2. Paul Connolly, *Navigating the Organizational Lifecycle: A Capacity Building Guide for Nonprofit Leaders* (Washington, DC: BoardSource, 2005), 4.

3. The theory on which the CCAT is based is the TCC Group's Four Core Capacities Model, which includes the following elements:

   • Leadership: the ability of all organizational leaders to create and sustain the vision, inspire, model, prioritize, make decisions, provide direction, and innovate, all in an effort to achieve the organizational mission

   • Adaptive: the ability of a nonprofit organization to monitor, assess, respond to, and create internal and external changes

   • Management: the ability of a nonprofit organization to ensure the effective and efficient use of organizational resources

   • Technical: the ability of a nonprofit organization to implement all of the key organizational and programmatic functions

   The CCAT measures a fifth area, *organizational culture,* defined as the context in which the core capacities operate.

CHAPTER TWO

1. Dan S. Cohen, *The Heart of Change Field Guide: Tools and Tactics for Leading Change in Your Organization* (Boston: Harvard Business School Press, 2005), 77.

2. Chip Heath and Dan Heath, *Switch: How to Change When Change Is Hard* (New York: Broadway Business, 2010), 156.

3. Susan Gross, *Seven Turning Points: Leading Through Pivotal Transitions in Organizational Life* (St. Paul, MN: Fieldstone Alliance, 2009), 59.

4. "Strategies for Change Leaders: A Conversation Between Peter F. Drucker and Peter M. Senge," in *On Leading Change,* eds. Frances Hesselbein and Rob Johnson (San Francisco: Jossey-Bass, 2002), 7–18.

5. BoardSource, *The Source: Twelve Principles of Governance That Power Exceptional Boards* (Washington, DC: BoardSource, 2005), 58.

6. Sadie Nash Leadership Project, "Philosophy," www.sadienash.org/about_us_philosophy.htm.

7. The New York Times Company Nonprofit Management Excellence Awards is a program that seeks to help nonprofit leaders improve the management of their organizations and inform all New Yorkers about management excellence in nonprofit organizations. The program represents a partnership between the New York Times Company Community Affairs Department, Philanthropy New York, and the Nonprofit Coordinating Committee of New York, which also manages the program.

CHAPTER THREE

1. Paul Connolly, *Navigating the Organizational Lifecycle: A Capacity Building Guide for Nonprofit Leaders* (Washington, DC: BoardSource, 2005), 20.

2. Susan Gross, *Seven Turning Points: Leading Through Pivotal Transitions in Organizational Life* (St. Paul, MN: Fieldstone Alliance, 2009), 22.

3. BoardSource, *The Source: Twelve Principles of Governance That Power Exceptional Boards* (Washington, DC: BoardSource, 2005).

4. Connolly, *Navigating,* 21.

5. BoardSource, *The Source,* 1.

6. Donelson R. Forsyth, *Group Dynamics,* 5th ed. (Belmont, CA: Wadsworth, Cengage Learning, 2009).

7. Gross, *Seven Turning Points.*

8. Edgar Schein, *Organizational Culture and Leadership*, 3rd ed. (San Francisco: Jossey-Bass, 2004).

9. Lee G. Bolman and Terrence E. Deal, *Reframing Organizations: Artistry, Choice, and Leadership*, 3rd ed. (San Francisco: Jossey-Bass, 2003).

CHAPTER FOUR

1. Peter York, *The Sustainability Formula: How Nonprofits Can Thrive in the Emerging Economy*, www.tccgrp.com/pdfs/SustainabilityFormula.pdf.

2. "Scaling Impact: Six Takeaways," *Evaluation Exchange* 15, no. 1 (Spring 2010): 24.

3. Grantmakers for Effective Organizations, *Topic 1: What Do We Mean by Scale?* February 2011, *GEO_SWW_WhatDoWeMeanbyScale_vFinal.pdf.*

4. ActKnowledge, "Theory of What?" July 11, 2011, www.theoryofchange .org/background/basics.html.

CHAPTER FIVE

1. Mitch McCrimmon, "Low Self Esteem," July 11, 2011, www.leadersdirect .com/low-self-esteem.

CHAPTER SIX

1. Judith Sharken Simon, *Five Life Stages of Nonprofit Organizations* (St. Paul, MN: Amherst D. Wilder Foundation, 2001).

2. Fred Mandell and Kathleen Jordan, *Becoming a Life Change Artist: 7 Creative Skills to Reinvent Yourself at Any Stage of Life.* (New York: Penguin Group, 2010).

3. Donna Weaver, "Surflight Theater in Beach Haven Needs $500,000 or Will Close by Halloween," pressofAtlanticCity.com, September 30, 2010, www .pressofatlanticcity.com/news/breaking/article_60e1f7aa-cbeb-11df-a944-001cc4c002e0.html.

4. Kym Klass, "Group Homes for Children Now Closed," *Montgomery Advertiser*, October 20, 2010, www.allbusiness.com/society-social/families-children-family/15215589-1.html.

5. Joe Marusak, "Riding Center's Closing Irks Longtime Supporters," CharlotteObserver.com, September 30, 2010, www.charlotteobserver .com/2010/09/30/1727354/riding-centers-closing-irks-longtime.html.

6. Ruth McCambridge, "Back to the Future: Paul Light's Recession Predictions Revisited," *Nonprofit Quarterly,* December 15, 2010, www.nonprofitquarterly .org/index.php?option=com_content&view=article&id=8071:back-to-the-future-paul-lights-recession-predictions-revisited&catid=153:features&Itemid=336.

7. Ron Mattock, *Zone of Insolvency* (Hoboken, NJ: Wiley, 2008); Kennard T. Wing, Thomas H. Pollak, and Amy Blackwood, *Nonprofit Almanac 2008* (Washington, DC: Urban Institute Press, 2008).

8. Nonprofit Finance Fund, 2010, http://nonprofitfinancefund.org/.

9. Richard Sims, National Education Association, www.nea.org/.

CHAPTER SEVEN

1. Peter York, *The Sustainability Formula: How Nonprofits Can Thrive in the Emerging Economy,* www.tccgrp.com/pdfs/SustainabilityFormula.pdf.

2. BoardSource, *The Source: Twelve Principles of Governance That Power Exceptional Boards* (Washington, DC: BoardSource, 2005), 1.

THE AUTHORS

John Brothers is a recognized leader in the nonprofit and philanthropic arena with over twenty years of sector experience and is a national expert in the field of executive leadership, nonprofit effectiveness, sustainability, and assisting organizations in both organizational growth and decline. Brothers gravitated toward nonprofit work as a result of his experiences growing up in poverty as a child in Minneapolis, Minnesota.

Brothers has a doctorate in law and policy from Northeastern University, an MPA in nonprofit management from New York University, and an MBA in public policy from American Public University, which he began at Columbia University. He has also studied at Georgetown University and the London School of Economics. He is an adjunct professor in social welfare policy at Rutgers University and in nonprofit management at New York University. Brothers recently served as a visiting scholar at the Hauser Center for Nonprofit Organizations at Harvard University and has had fellowships with the Higher Education Consortium for Urban Affairs and the Children's Defense Fund.

Brothers is also the editor of the *Journal for Nonprofit Management* in his role as a senior fellow with the Support Center for Nonprofit Management. Brothers is a popular blogger with the *Stanford Social Innovation Review* and recently collaborated on a book on nonprofit leadership with SAGE Publications. He has been interviewed, referenced, or quoted in dozens of local, regional, national, and international media outlets, including *The Chronicle of Philanthropy, Crain's Business, The Washington Post, Newsweek (Japan Edition)*, ABC News, the *New York Post*, and *The Wall Street Journal*.

Brothers, a Certified Fund Raising Executive (CFRE), is also the principal of Cuidiu Consulting, a consulting firm servicing nonprofit, philanthropic, and government efforts throughout the United States and internationally. Cuidiu Consulting has contracted with hundreds of organizations, and Brothers has trained or spoken to thousands of people in all areas of philanthropy, public policy, capacity building, and organizational development.

Brothers is married with two young children and lives outside of New York City in New Jersey.

Anne Sherman is the director of strategy at TCC Group, a consultancy that assists nonprofits, foundations, and corporate community involvement programs. She has worked with dozens of organizations on strategic planning, business planning, organizational assessment, and evaluation and other types of capacity building engagements. Prior to joining TCC Group, Sherman served as community initiatives manager and special projects coordinator at Minneapolis Way To Grow.

Sherman holds a master's degree in public affairs from the University of Minnesota Hubert H. Humphrey Institute for Public Affairs and is a graduate of Haverford College. She also completed graduate course work in community health education at the University of Minnesota's School of Public Health. She currently chairs the advisory board of the Center for Family Life in Sunset Park, Brooklyn, and sits on the board of SCO Family of Services.

INDEX

Page references followed by *fig* indicate an illustrated figure; followed by *t* indicate a table.

challenges, 71; on leadership, 70, 71; on management, 70; on manager-to-staff communication, 71; on organizational culture, 71; on technical skills, 71

Center for Human Environments, 95

Challenges: CCAT findings on core program, 42; CCAT findings on infrastructure phase, 71; of the decline phase, 104; MIE phase resource development, 76, 162

Change: ability to adapt dependent on leadership, 30–31; achieving the mission by understanding, 160–161; authors' perspective on need for, 10–11; evolving infrastructure phase board facilitating, 61–63; lifecycle used as framework for, 3–10*fig*; motivation of agents of, 21; as nonprofit constant, 1–2; shifting organizational DNA, 133–140; Theory of Change (TOC) development process for, 94–95; trust required for, 31–33; vision statement as effective tool for, 18. *See also* Turnaround phase

Change agent motivation, 21

Charlotte Observer, 140

Chicago Public Schools, 98

Christian Activity Center (CAC): description and accomplishment of, 38; extraordinary assistance provided to, 38; leadership role in evolution of, 41; process of transformation at, 38–39; stakeholder engagement in mission and values of, 39–40; on the true "core" of, 40–41

Churchill, Winston, 56

City University of New York, 95

Clinton, Monte, 153

Closing organization mind-set: acceptance, 145; anger, 142–143; bargaining, 143–144; denial, 142; depression, 144

Closing organizations: downward apex point prior to, 129*fig*–130; economic crisis (2008) increase of, 140–141; historical look at lifecycle thought on, 128; mind-set of, 141–145; understanding the, 127. *See also* Turnaround phase

CME Group Foundation, 98

Cohen, Dan S., 18

Collins, Jim, 134

Communication: CCAT findings on infrastructure stage, manager-to-staff, 71; CCAT findings on MIE phase, manager-to-staff, 101; development of core competencies in, 53–54; as self-awareness requirement, 31

Community partners: building relationships with, 80; how a crisis may impact, 117–119

Complacency signs: dwindling passion for the mission, 116–117; "it ain't broke," 114–115; macro, macro, and more macro, 115–116; trusting to a fault, 113–114

Connolly, Paul, 46, 58

Core program interviews: Christian Activity Center (CAC), 38–41; Sadie Nash Leadership Project, 34–37

Harvard Family Research Project, 94

The Heart of Change Field Guide (Cohen), 18

Heath, Chip, 21

Heath, Dan, 21

High-arc organization decline phase: cash flow management during, 107; description of, 105–106; enhancing board bench strength during, 107; mind-set during, 108–112; scenario planning during, 107–108*fig*

High-arc organizations: decline phase of, 105–112; infrastructure or adolescence phase of, 46–47; maturity/impact expansion (MIE) phase of, 74–75*fig*, 112; trajectories of, 9*fig*, 106. *See also* Organizations

Hijacked boards, 59–61

Holloway, Sarah, 96

Human capital: CSE impact area, 90; economic crisis impacting, 117. *See also* Staff; Volunteers

Hurricane Katrina, 23

I

Infrastructure or adolescence phase: Becky James-Hatter of BBBSEMO interview, 67–70; board-ED relationship during, 56–58; CCAT findings on, 70–71; clear articulation of values during, 64–65; consequences of hijacked board during, 59–61; consequences of a weak board during, 58–59; description of, 45–46; evolving board during, 61–63; organizational culture during, 46, 63–67; planning for organizational

growth, 48–55; rate of growth during the, 47; role of the board during, 55–63

Innovation value, 65

Internal leadership: CCAT findings on infrastructure phase, 70; CCAT findings on MIE phase, 101

The International Who's Who of Music, 121

Interviews: Becky James-Hatter of BBBSEMO, 67–70; Carole Wacey of MOUSE, 95–100; Christian Activity Center (CAC), 38–41; Sadie Nash Leadership Project, 34–37; Thomas Wolf, 120–125

"It ain't broke" problem: description of, 114; solution to, 114–115

J

James-Hatter, Becky, 67–70

Jordan, Kathleen, 134

K

Kennedy Center, 121

King, Martin Luther, Jr., 153

Kingsdorf, Pastor Klaus, 153

Kübler-Ross, Elisabeth, 142

L

Leader influence, 101

Leader vision: CCAT findings on core program, 42; CCAT findings on infrastructure phase, 70; CCAT findings on MIE phase, 101. *See also* Vision

Leadership: ability to adapt dependent on, 30–31; CCAT findings on core program, 42; CCAT findings on infrastructure phase, 70; CCAT findings on MIE phase, 101; CSE tool for diversifying,

161; values statement of, 14, 19–24; vision of, 14, 17–19. *See also* Mission; Organizations

Nuzum, John, 154, 155

O

On Death and Dying (Kübler-Ross), 142

Organization DNA shift: applying discipline for, 138–139; collaborating for, 137–138; embracing uncertainty and taking risks, 136–137; Main Street Services (MSS) case studies on, 135–140; preparing for the, 134–135; seeing new perspectives for, 135–136; turnaround through, 133–134. *See also* Organizational culture

Organization lifecycle: change as a constant in, 1–2; core program phase, 13–43; decline phase of, 103–125, 162; as framework for change, 3–10*fig*; infrastructure or adolescence phase, 45–71; knowing where you are to get where you want to go premise of, 163; maturity/impact expansion (MIE) phase, 73–102, 112, 162; turnaround or closing phase, 127–158, 162–163; understanding the journey continues past "top" of, 162. *See also* Stevens Lifecycle model; TCC Group model

Organizational capacity: CCAT findings on core program, 41–43; CCAT findings on infrastructure/adolescence phase, 70–71; CCAT findings on maturity/impact expansion (MIE), 100–102; four gas tanks metaphor of, 145–147; funder incentives for building, 151–152; regular

assessments of five key elements of, 148–149

Organizational capacity key elements: board of directors performance, 148; executive director performance, 148; financial position and effectiveness of business model, 148–149; market analysis, 148; staff performance evaluations, 149

Organizational complacency signs: dwindling passion for the mission, 116–117; "it ain't broke," 114–115; macro, macro, and more macro, 115–116; trusting to a fault, 113–114

Organizational culture: of BBBSEMO's accountability core of, 68–69; CCAT findings on core program, 43; CCAT findings on infrastructure phase, 71; CCAT findings on MIE phase, 102; including "nonnegotiables" in, 65–66; infrastructure phase development of, 63–67; need for infrastructure requiring shift in, 46; understanding and developing your, 162. *See also* Organizational DNA shift

Organizational Culture and Leadership (Schein), 64

Organizational growth: achieving the mission by understanding, 160–161; adaptive leadership as key to sustainable, 161; defining nature and meaning of, 160; of high-arc organizations, 106; issues related to rate of, 47; low-arc organization trajectories, 10*fig*; management to support, 52–54; program expansion, 48–52; sustainability issues

mission and strategy, 17; of start-up organizations, 19. *See also* Leader vision

Vision statements: as effective change management tool, 18; functions of, 17–18

Volunteers: impact of economic crisis on programs for, 119; leveraging time and skills of, 152. *See also* Human capital

W

Wacey, Carole, 95–100

Wagner College, 153

Wagner School of Public Service (New York University), 141

Weak boards, 58–59

West, Phil, 152–153

Wolf, Thomas, 120–125

WolfBrown, 120

Y

YMCA, 94

York, Peter, 6, 30, 76–77

Z

Zone of Insolvency (Mattock), 141